GOD'S LOVE
FOR THE SHAMEFUL

GOD'S LOVE

FOR THE SHAMEFUL

*Feeding the Heart, Mind, and
Soul with the Truth*

Jesus answered.

Beverly D. Wiebe

iUniverse, Inc.
Bloomington

God's Love for the Shameful
Feeding the Heart, Mind, and Soul with the Truth

iUniverse books may be ordered through booksellers or by contacting:

iUniverse
1663 Liberty Drive
Bloomington, IN 47403
www.iuniverse.com
1-800-Authors (1-800-288-4677)

ISBN: 978-1-4759-4501-0 (sc)
ISBN: 978-1-4759-4503-4 (hc)
ISBN: 978-1-4759-4502-7 (ebk)

Printed in the United States of America

iUniverse rev. date: 08/22/2012

CONTENTS

ACKNOWLEDGEMENTS

Praise goes to my God whom has been the writer through me. God has truly brought me on a journey that ended up bringing glory to him.

My deepest gratitude goes to my wonderful husband Garry whom is my closest friend. Thank you for your unending love and support. You were behind me from the very beginning in my career to write. Without your encouragement Garry this book could not have been written. To my children Brandon and Brooke, who provided me with hugs as I went off to write in peace and quite. My gratitude to my wonderful parents whom have loved me and raised me with the values that I hold on to today and have taught me to follow God with all my heart, soul and mind. My gratitude goes to my sister Colleen and brother Steven whom has always given me encouragement through their walk with God. I want to express a special thanks to Lili who through this journey, I have built a special friendship with. Thanks for your kind words when I so needed them. You listened on as I expressed my thoughts. All are dearly loved and treasured in my heart. God Bless. My thanks goes to I-universe for there guidance in the process of publishing my book.

INTRODUCTION

From my heart to yours I am delighted to tell you how the love of God has transformed me. This book is written to inspire and motivate one whom wants to live a life of freedom. The challenges, frustration and failures of life can be overwhelming and confusing. This book is to to help you understand who you truly are through Gods love. There is power in the word of God. I have included many scriptures from the NIV translation Bible. It is through the word of God that has brought a transformation into my life.

I struggled through school, trying to find my path in life. Wanting to be with the in crowd. I found myself looking in all the wrong places for my happiness. Weekend parties and hanging out at bars is where I found it easy to release the stresses of life. At the time I did not see the path of disaster that I was creating for myself.

Divorced at the age of twenty two, looking for a new place to call home with no career.

The fears and doubts of who I was overwhelmed me. Questions of "Who am I" and "Where is God?" I let my shameful experiences lead me into a deep depression that kept me locked in a dark place.

One night as I was crying myself to sleep, an overwhelming sensation of bright light consumed the room. The light gave off an overpowering knowledge that I was loved. Through the warm sensation of this light came knowledge that I was going to be ok. The shadows of darkness within me were being cleansed. The light was peaceful. The light had overpowered the darkness within. I wanted the warmth and security of the light to stay. I knew that this experience was God. I wanted to know how to keep this very experience of God alive.

Within the next two years of searching for God, and his presence in my life, I was able to trust again.

Remarried in June of 1997 to my husband Garry. After, the birth of our first son in 1999, I woke up one morning with the overpowering sensation to write a book and to name it Gods Love for The Shameful.

I spoke of it to my husband that morning. I dismissed the idea. I struggled with the fact that I was not good enough to write a book. I allowed the shameful experiences in my life to dictate to me once again of my self worth. I realized that I was allowing my imperfections stop me from living a life I was intended to have from the very beginning.

My son now thirteen, and the thought of Gods whisper to write this book had been with me all these years. I rejected Gods Love, and instead became more shameful.

I discovered the love of God from letting go of my shame, and not allowing it to dictate to me anymore. I was choosing to hang on to the shame of all my past failures.

When I chose to let Gods love in the most amazing transformation took place. Gods love overpowered the shame that overwhelmed me. Gods love allowed me to choose life, instead of allowing life to happen to me. Gods love is the path to true freedom.

Gods love is the key that has opened up the door to the Kingdom of Heaven.

Gods love has blessed me in my marriage, my work, my finances and my friendships. I have never looked back. I now carry the key to life.

The Glory belongs to our Father in Heaven. Amen.

TRUTH

Jesus said to the people who believed in him, "You are truly my disciples if you keep obeying my teachings. And you will know the truth, and the truth will set you free." John 8:31-32

The pain that people go through is brought on by their own choices, I realized I was allowing my own choices to destroy me. I was letting my past, and the experiences in my life dictate to me who I was. I also realized that I was not alone, there are so many of us hurting in our world and are living a life of ignorance. Another way to put it lost in a matrix.

I realized that I was getting stronger when I awakened myself to the truth. I was lost in the thoughts that consumed me from living a good life. I was suffering in all that I do. The choices I make now, are affecting my tomorrow. The dominant thoughts that I have are shaping my life. I wanted understanding in all of this, and chose to let my new life begin. I found Gods love for the shameful.

The definition of freedom is different for all of us. Every time I would think of freedom, I was bombarded by thoughts of how hard it is to find or impossible to have. I became frustrated with reality. Freedom was so far away.

I discovered that freedom comes from within. It is our thoughts that keep us from the freedom that we so desire. Our ego gets in the way, and dictates to us through our fears and anxieties.

I want others to know they can live in freedom. Like I said freedom is different for all of us. It is up to us as an individual to define what freedom means to us.

Jesus died for our sins. Which freed us from our sins. Jesus paid the price for our freedom.

I was keeping myself locked up in the sin. My dominant thought was on the shame of the sin. Jesus paid the price when he died. Why was I keeping myself focused on the sins.

I became fascinated with God as he opened up my mind. We are to love God with all our heart, mind and soul.

We are to fill our mind with thoughts that are pure and lovely. Thoughts that are good for your mind.

In scripture:

And now, dear brothers and sisters, one final thing. Fix your thoughts on what is true, and honorable, and right, and pure, and lovely, and admirable. Think about things that are excellent and worthy of praise. Phillipians 4:8

Our ego is a false centre that keeps us from the very freedom we already have. The freedom that Jesus had already died for.

The mind is broken down in the following our conscious and our subconscious. We choose our thoughts from our conscious. From our conscious we filter to our subconscious. Our belief system is then held in our subconscious that works all the time. There is no down time for the subconscious mind.

Our subconscious is always on autopilot. Our subconscious mind stores all of our previous life experiences, your beliefs, your memories, your skills, all situation you've been through and all images you've ever seen. Our feelings are triggered from the subconscious mind. Our beliefs are stored in the subconscious mind, by our conscious thoughts. What is your belief?

When we have an experience in our life good, or bad, they become programmed within our minds.

There are things that we would like to forget about and not think about. We try to push them away and not think about them. They may go out of conscious mind, but remain in our subconscious mind. Remember, our subconscious mind stores all our previous life experiences. What you believe guides you.

We must learn to keep our mind clear. It means to forgive others. We will go deeper regarding forgiveness later on in the book.

Jesus was very clear regarding our conscious. In scripture he spoke on our thought life.

In Scripture:

And then he added, "It is the thought-life that defiles you. For from within, out of a person's heart, come evil thoughts, sexual immorality, theft, murder, adultery, greed, wickedness, deceit, eagerness for lustful pleasure, envy, slander, pride, and foolishness. All these vile things come from within: they are what defile you and make you unacceptable to God." Mark 7:20-23

Jesus warns us to keep our thought life pure. Jesus did this to protect us and to help us to stay in a right relationship with God. The experiences that have brought moments of shame into our life from sin can destroy us. They are programmed in our subconscious mind.

Our thought life builds our Kingdom within us. Jesus was very clear that our thought life defiles us. We build through Jesus our heart, mind, and soul with what is true and worthy.

In my youth I made choices that I was not proud of, and as I continued to make choices it lead me down the wide path.

In Scripture:

"You can enter God's Kingdom only through the narrow gate. The highway to hell is broad, and its gate is wide for the many who choose that way. But the gateway to life is

3

very narrow and the road is difficult, and only a few ever find it." Matthew 7:13-14

When we live by Gods ways which are acceptable to him, we keep our conscience clear. We do this by allowing Jesus into our hearts. It is only through Jesus whom lived a sin free life can we come to God. Jesus accomplished the will of God, and that makes him right with God. That is why Jesus now sits at the right side of God in Heaven.

I did not respect myself as a young woman, and through not respecting myself I was ashamed. When I did not respect myself, I than had been filled with thoughts in my mind that I started then to battle. Through my negative thought pattern I had brought painful relationship's into my life. The negative thoughts give off bad feelings, which brought more negative experiences into my life. It becomes a vicious circle. I let my thought life defile me.

I searched for happiness in my relationships, which led me to a painful divorce. At the time I was angry at my ex-husband and blamed him for all my grief. I was in pain and felt all alone. I had blamed him for my misery.

When I parted from that relationship, I wanted him to pay for all my misery. I wanted him to have a miserable life. I wanted revenge.

When we let experiences in our life take over through our thoughts we end up destroying our being. We must live a conscience free life.

In Scripture:

They demonstrate that God's law is written in their hearts, for their own conscience and thought either accuse them or tell them they are doing right. Romans 2:15

I had chosen not to live by Gods laws. I fell into the trap of what sin can do. When we are living a life that is not God honouring we are not allowed into the kingdom. My choices were keeping me out of the Kingdom.

In Scripture:

> *But the Holy Spirit produces this kind of fruit in our lives: love, joy, peace, patience, kindness, goodness, faithfulness, gentleness, and self-control. There is no law against these things! Those who belong to Christ Jesus have nailed the passions and desires of their sinful nature to his cross an crucified them there. Since we are living by the Spirit, let us follow the Spirit's leading in every part of our lives. Let us not become conceited, or provoke one another, or be jealous of one another. Galations 5:22-26*

When we make a choice to be guided by God and surround ourselves in his love, we gain the Kingdom.

As the above scripture in Galations tells us two clear paths we are allowed to choose. God gives us a choice, explaining to us which one leads to his Kingdom. This is the free will of God. Live his will or yours.

The kingdom is only for the person whom chooses to have a deeper relationship with God. Now, when we decide to choose walking Gods path, we must clear what is in us. We must clear our conscious. We can not overcome it alone.

God made everything good. When we read in the beginning of scripture in Genesis the first book of the bible it walks us through God creating the universe. All of Gods creation was good. It is us that corrupts our thoughts in the way we live. It is our thought life that defiles us.

We are keeping ourselves from the Kingdom of the choices we make. When you want to know God, and seek his ways he will show you his will for you.

When I found God's love it is then that I realized, I needed him more than anything. I knew I needed him because I was not satisfied in life. I wanted to live. I wanted freedom. There is freedom with God.

We choose what direction we want to go. When we choose the narrow path we are choosing the correct path. This is the path that is less ventured, but reaps the most benefit.

I want you to understand when you choose to cling on to the past. An experience that has brought shame, by a choice you made. You are locking the door to great things. When we ask God to help us let go, by admitting our sin, and asking for truth in our life he will show us. Gods will for us is to have freedom.

I am here to tell you that you are allowed to live a life of joy, peace, and abundance. I am here to tell you that it is offered to everyone, and it is a matter of choice. Gods love for the shameful has no limits.

When you realize that the choices you have made in your life is why you are where you are in life. You can change it by recognizing the truth.

We are intended to live a life of happiness. We all get to have a good life. We are intended to live life to the fullest.

Whatever it is in your life that brought you to the place where you are right now, you can change it from this moment on. I want you to know that your life is meant for living. Living a life with peace.

Gods love will bring you closer to the creator who designed you, to walk with him the way you were intended to from the very beginning. We are called to live a life of abundance of joy, peace, and happiness. We are called to experience life to the fullest.

When God lives in you, it is his desire for you to get to know him so you can experience the love he has for you, and through that love he will reveal the real you, and you will discover the greatest gifts he has for each and everyone who chooses him.

In these next chapters I write the many areas that bring us into the state of mind that sin empowers us. Through the power of Jesus Christ you will be forever changed when you allow the chains of sin to be released and bring in all of what Jesus Christ has to offer.

Jesus is truly the way to a life of freedom and abundance with God. Jesus died on the cross to release us from the grips of sin. His blood cleanses us from the inside.

Gods love is the power that breaks the chains of sin.

In scripture:

Therefore, since we are surrounded by such a huge crowd of witnesses to the life of faith, let us strip off every weight that slows us down, especially the sin that so easily trip us up. And let us run with endurance the race God has set before us. We do this by keeping our eyes on Jesus, the champion who initiates and perfects our faith. Because of the joy awaiting him, he endured the cross, disregarding its shame. Now he is seated in the place of honour beside God's throne. Think of all the hostility he endured from sinful people: then you won't become weary and give up. After all, you have not yet given your lives in your struggle against sin. Hebrews 12:1-4

God says we are the most valuable of his creation. We are all different and unique which means that God is very creative.

In scripture:

Not even a sparrow, worth only half a penny, can fall to the ground without your Father knowing it. And the very hairs on your head are all numbered. So don't be afraid; you are more valuable to him than a whole flock of sparrows. Matthew 10:29-31

God cares for each one of us. He knows each one of us personally. He created us in his image. God is creative. God is also omnipresent which means he is everywhere. God is Omniscient which means God is all knowing. God is also omnipotence which means God is all powerful. Omni is the universal attribute of God. We can not hide from God, he fills the universe. This is important and valuable knowledge. Knowing God is the strength of our lives. Knowing God gives us direction and focus in our lives.

When a person believes they acknowledge his presence, and we grow in our relationship with him. God desires us to have a relationship with him. Our ego, and hardened heart stand in the way.

God sees our hearts. When we are humble to God we are submitting ourselves to him. When we are humble our ego gets smaller and our heart grows. God knows a sincere heart.

We are to keep our focus on Jesus. He overcame sin. He overcame the shame of the world. He did it, because he chose to do it.

How do we close the gap between us and God. We can't, it is impossible for us alone. That is why he sent his son Jesus to die for us. Jesus carried the sin of the world when he died, and conquered death so we can live for eternity with God. Jesus is Gods love for the shameful.

Gods love for us is stronger than you can imagine, and it is through the grace of his love that we are saved.

In scripture:

> *Those who are dominated by the sinful nature think about sinful things, but those who are controlled by the Holy Spirit think about things that please the Spirit. If your sinful nature controls you mind, there is death. But if the Holy Spirit controls your mind, there is life and peace. For the sinful nature is always hostile to God. It never did obey God's laws, and it never will. That's why those who are still under the control of their sinful nature, can never please God. Romans 8:5-8*

The above verse in scripture tells that if we are dominated by our sinful nature we are doomed. There is death. When the Holy Spirit controls our mind there is life and peace.

The Holy Spirit comes from knowing God. When we want to come to know God, we come through his son Jesus. Jesus died for us so we can come in confidence to God. We are bought out of sin from the death of Jesus.

Only through Jesus can we be forgiven from sin. It is through Jesus that we are freed from shame. Shame has no power over your thoughts when you focus on Jesus. The death of Jesus conquered our sins. Jesus came for the shameful. Jesus came to save us.

When we live a life focused on Jesus we are given the Holy Spirit from Jesus. When we live in truth of who Jesus is we enter the Kingdom of Heaven which we carry within us. The Kingdom is near said Jesus. He was talking about us keeping our thoughts focused on him. We have access to the Kingdom of Heaven through him.

When we are far from God in our journey through life, we tend to fall in the traps of the world. We make decisions that lead us down a wrong path, that brings hardships, and trials. We are given free will to choose.

Our love from God was sent in his son Jesus. Jesus was sent to the earth for a purpose. His purpose was to bring us back to God. Jesus was bringing us back to the Kingdom of Heaven.

Living under Jesus authority was not to condemn us, but to deliver us into freedom. He came to guide us to truth.

Jesus taught many during his time here on earth, and performed many miracles. Jesus had forgiven many sins, and his desire was for others to follow him. He taught many crowds, and spent a lot of time with his disciples which were followers of his. The twelve disciples that he taught had brought the message through the nations over billions of years until today to our generation. The Bible is the word of God. The word of God is to guide us, not to hinder us. The Bible is all of Gods Truth, and is key to developing a relationship with him.

Jesus taught his disciples to spread the word about who he is, and that he is the King, and Salvation for all who choose to believe. Jesus wants there to be no more separation between us and God. He honoured Gods plan, and lived his life according to the will of God. That is why God gave him the inheritance to the kingdom of heaven.

In scripture:

For God so loved the world that he gave his one and only
Son, that whoever believes in him shall not perish but have
eternal life. John 3:16

God loves us so much that he sacrificed his only son. God's love for us is more than we can ever imagine.

From the very beginning God created us in his image, and man sinned against God. We were separated from God by our own choices. We could not be in his presence. Gods unconditional love has given us a gift of his only son. To believe in him. To come to the cross, and humble ourselves to him. Admit we are a sinner, and ask for forgiveness. When we do this we Glorify God, and bring him into our lives so we can now have a right relationship with God. We then live with God for eternity.

To truly seek God with all your heart, mind and soul you will enter into a relationship with him through Jesus. We then are welcomed in to the family of God, and called his children. We become heirs to the Kingdom of Heaven when we believe in Jesus.

God tells us in scripture that when we seek him with all our heart, mind, and soul we will receive understanding, knowledge and wisdom. They are the keys to life.

Gods love for the shameful, is to understand that God came down to earth through Jesus. Jesus took the shame of the world and went through the humiliation of being hung on the cross and died for our sins. Jesus did it because he knew that you and I could not pay for our own sins. Nothing is impossible to God.

It is not by your works that you are saved, it was by the grace of God that you are saved. We must accept the gift of Jesus to enter the Kingdom of Heaven.

Glory to God for his love.

FAILURE

At that moment the Lord turned and looked at Peter. Then Peter remembered that the Lord had said, "Before the rooster crows tomorrow morning, you will deny me three times." And Peter left the courtyard, crying bitterly. Luke 22:61-62

The above verse grips me when I think of what Peter must have been going through. To look into the eyes of Jesus, right after you deny him not once, not twice, but three times. When in fact the Lord had predicted this the night before. The stare must have felt like eternity.

The failure of not having Jesus' back at that moment must have been painful. We read that Peter left crying bitterly.

Is that not what we do. We hurt. We struggle with the pain if only I can do it all over again. Failure is something we try to avoid all together. When we fail we have so many feelings and emotions that overcome us. That they overwhelm us. Often we allow the negative feelings that come from failure shape us.

In Scripture:

As the Scriptures say, "No one is good—not even one. No one has real understanding: no one is seeking God. Romans 3:10

We can not escape it on our own, we need to have Jesus help us through it.

We read that Peter had fought failure when he denied Jesus Christ.

In scripture:

So they arrested him and led him to the high priest's residence, and Peter was following far behind. The guards lit a fire in the courtyard and sat around it, and Peter joined them there.

A servant girl noticed him in the firelight and began staring at him. Finally she said, "this man was one of Jesus' followers!".

Peter denied it. "Woman," he said, "I don't even know the man!"

After awhile someone else looked at him and said, "You must be one of them!"

"No, man, I'm not!" Peter replied.

About an hour later someone else insisted" this must be one of Jesus disciples because he is a Galilean, too." But Peter said, "Man, I don't know what you are talking about." And as soon as he said these words, the rooster crowed.

At that moment the Lord turned and looked at Peter. Then Peter remembered that the Lord had said. "Before the rooster crows tomorrow morning, you will deny me three times." And Peter left the courtyard, crying bitterly. Luke 22:54-62

Failure can lead to backsliding and letting go of Jesus all together. In the resentment of our despair we can be lead into a path that can lead to even more troubles. It is how we handle our failures that is important, not the failure itself.

Peter had denied his own weakness in Matthew 26:33 to Jesus. The Bible warns us to be careful that we don't fall into sin.

In scripture:

"If you think you are standing strong be careful for you too may fall into the same sin". 1 Corinthians 10:12

In order to overcome failure we need to pray. We need to come to God through Jesus Christ. Our hearts and our mind need to be continued to be cleansed. We do that by having a relationship with God through Jesus.

Jesus predicted that Peter was going to deny Him and instructed Peter to pray while Jesus was in the Garden of Gethsemane.

In scripture:

Then Jesus brought them to an olive grove called Gethsemane, and he said, "sit her while go on ahead to pray." He took Peter and Zebedee's two sons, James and John, and he began to be filled with anguish and deep distress. He told them, "My soul is crushed with grief to the point of death. Stay here and watch with me." He went on a little farther and fell face down on the ground, "My Father! If it is possible, let this cup of suffering be taken away from me. Yet I want your will, not mine." Then He returned to the disciples and found them asleep. He said to Peter, "Couldn't you stay awake and watch with me even one hour? Keep alert and pray. Otherwise temptation will overpower you. For through the spirit is willing enough, the body is weak!" Again He left them and prayed, "My Father! If this cup cannot be taken away until I drink it, your will be done." He returned to

*them again and found them sleeping, for they just couldn't
keep their eyes open. Matthew 26:36-43*

If we are prayerless we become weak into temptation. In fact
being prayerless is a sin, because God has instructed us to pray.

Prayer is what keeps us close to God. We grow in a close
relationship through our quiet time with God. Failures show us the
need for Jesus.

When God is active in your life through Jesus, and you have a
life of active prayers flowing through your every day routine, when
disaster hits there is a sense of peace, because you draw on your
faith in God. That is what God does for us in our relationship with
him. It is our choice to acknowledge him and to have him live out
through us.

Reading the word of God, praying, meeting with other believers
by going to church are what God asks of us. He does not want to
hinder us, he wants to build us up.

The Love of God in a person is shown by how they respond
to everyday situations. You see Peter followed from a distance. He
became cold and was attracted to the fire. He denied Christ when
the rooster crowed three times and hid in the crowds of people. His
fear was stronger than his love for Jesus.

In scripture

*Oh the joys of those who do not follow the advise of the
wicked, or stand around with sinners, or join in with
mockers. Psalm 1:1*

When we lose focus on God, we end up listening to our sinful
nature side and do as Peter did and have little faith.

When the passion in our heart dies the fire for Jesus Christ will
grow cold, and we look to other places for warmth. When Peter
denied Christ it says he began to curse and swear. Peter lost himself
and the awareness of God.

Despite Peters fall he was restored when his eyes met Jesus. When Peter met the eyes of Jesus it says he cried bitterly. He grieved over his sin. Jesus saw his heart. The bible says that "God can use sorrow in our lives to help us turn away from sin and seek salvation".

In Scripture:

For God can use sorrow in our lives to help us turn away from sin and seek salvation. We will never regret that kind of sorrow. But sorrow without repentance is the kind that results to death. 2 Corinthians 7:10

After the resurrection of Jesus an angel appeared to Mary with a message to his disciples, including Peter (Mark 16:7) Jesus wanted Peter to know he still loved him. Jesus made it clear to include Peter, because he saw his heart and knew what Peter felt after he denied him. He saw the shame he felt, he saw the failure he felt.

Jesus can see the heart, and he wants us to know even when we fail, we can come back to him.

In scripture:

Now go and tell his disciples, including Peter, that Jesus is going ahead of you to Galilee. You will see him there, just as he told you before he died." Mark 16:7

We will all fail or sin in our life. We are only fooling ourselves and refusing to accept the truth. When we sin we need to run to, not away from Jesus.

Do not let failure shape you and lead you away from God. Learn from it, and let God help you to let go of the negative thoughts that come from failure.

When Peter let go and learned from his failure, God used him in extraordinary ways.

Peter changed his attitude when he let God do his work through him.

God saw the heart of Peter when Jesus looked at him that moment he had denied him three times. Jesus saw the anguish in his heart.

When we look at the story of how Peter went on to do the work for God, you see how God can change a person even from a shameful moment in their life. God lifts up the weak and shows them that they are valuable, and worthy to him. God loves everyone, and it is through our failures that he teaches us.

When we fail in life it is our reaction afterwards that makes a turning point in our life. When we fail at something and learn from our mistake we grow. Without growth in our lives we cannot cannot become stronger. It truly is a part of life. We must learn from our failures.

Thank you Jesus for showing us how perfect your way is.

REJECTION

Then Jesus asked them, "didn't you ever read this in the scriptures? "The Stone that builders rejected has now become the cornerstone. This is the Lord's doing and it is wonderful to see." Matthew 21:42

How does God know anything about rejection? How can he possibly understand what I am going through? He just does not get it!

God does get it, and he understands. We all have been rejected in our life. Whatever the case may be, rejection does not feel good. No one likes to be rejected. What we do with that rejection is what changes everything.

I had been rejected in many areas of my life and I can tell you it did not feel good. Being rejected always comes with negative thoughts. What did I do wrong? What could I have done differently? How could I have got them to accept me? Do you see the bad thoughts that can be planted?

These are the seeds that Jesus refers to in the bible. The seeds that are the thoughts that we are planting within ourselves.

Jesus warns us to store our treasures in heaven. Wherever your treasure is your heart and thoughts will also be.

The feeling of being rejected makes a person feel inadequate.

In a relationship with Jesus, you grow to understand that he was rejected from the world. The world did not want him. The world rejected perfection. Why did so many hate this man and not want to listen to his teachings? They were lead inside by their fears of the unknown. They chose Jesus to be crucified over a criminal. Jesus was a perfect man with no sin and was sent to die on the cross. He died for our sin, he died for our shame.

Jesus stood for Truth. Jesus was pure and holy. Truth that is our abundance. The people that lived when Jesus walked the earth had rejected truth. Which in fact they closed themselves off from living in freedom.

When we come to know Jesus we will see the Power of Jesus Christ. We will be shown the abundance in life that we are all given. Everyone is given an equal share.

Jesus, was brought into this world through God whom planned this from the very beginning of creation. Jesus was born to virgin Mary. The purpose of Jesus was to save the world. Jesus was to be sacrificed for you and I. To die for our sin. To conquer death, because without Jesus we were all subject to die. Jesus closed the gap between you and God that sin holds us in. The shame from sin digs deep within us.

Even not admitting you're a sinner is a sin in itself. We are all born of sin, and are imperfect. Our human nature is to sin. Holding onto shame, distances us from God.

When you are born into this world. You are born into an imperfect world. You are given choices, and the choices you make shapes your life. You are influenced by your parents, family, teachers and friends. You choose what you believe, and it is through those choices that you begin your story in life. The choice is free will.

Now, when Jesus was sacrificed, he bought our lives back with his blood. We are given a choice to follow Jesus whom is the light of the world. Jesus stands for truth, and died for us so we can be saved from this world.

The opposite of light is darkness. Choices we make can lead to live in darkness. The darkness stems from sin. We are in fact rejecting Truth.

When we choose Jesus the light we are in fact rejecting the ways of the world. Jesus brings us on a path of truth, and he draws in the gap that keeps us from having a personal relationship with God. When we sacrifice ourselves to Jesus, by laying ourselves at the foot of the cross we are open for God to do the greatest work in us. The way we lay ourselves at the cross, is to recognize that we are a sinner. We humble ourselves by recognizing who Jesus is. Jesus is the son of God. Living for Jesus we are transformed to see through the ways of the world.

Now, let me explain when I say we do not live by the ways of this world. That does not mean you don't have to pay taxes, or get to drive any speed you desire. Yes, you must abide by the earthly laws. The difference what the world offers are not going to bring truth and purpose into your life.

Look around you at what the world offers you. What we watch on TV, the movies we watch, the advertising we see on billboards, magazines we read, and the music we listen too, The messages we get from the world are we need to have the best house, the best car, the best clothes. Even if you don't like the way you look you can change it by plastic surgery. The messages the world gives is to change the physical. The world does not offer the true message of life. The truth is found in Jesus Christ.

When we look for joy and happiness in the world we fall into traps of Satan's lies. Satan is known to be the prince of darkness, or the prince of this world. It is then that the thought of rejection can shape us. If we are always trying to live by the standard of the world which is to live by the physical realm. Then we can make the mistake and allow the thoughts of rejection from the world to shape us.

When Jesus is the centre of our lives we are rooted in truth. We are lead down the right path.

Through looking in wrong places I found my husband through world circumstances. I met my husband at a time in my life where Jesus was not important to me. I found a man that did not have a love for Jesus, and whom did not share that deep desire with in me to follow the ways of God.

I had knowledge of Jesus but I did not have depth in my relationship with him. Without a deep relationship with Jesus, I had not been walking a close relationship with God.

I was looking in the wrong places to make me feel complete. I was not grounded in who I was, and I was looking for myself in another person.

Joy is found in Jesus Christ. No other relationship can fulfill you. It is impossible for an earthly relationship to complete you. Jesus Christ can complete you. Jesus will never reject you.

God is the only one that can complete us. We can not expect another to do that for us, that is why so many relationships are destined to fall apart before they even begin. When another does not meet our needs, we tend to bring friction or pull away from the other in resentment.

When Jesus says do not conform your ways to this world, he means that we are not to live our life according to the way of the world. What the world has to offer brings us into emotions that bring sadness, anger, envy and fear.

In scripture Jesus told his disciples how to be truly happy.

In scripture:

God blesses those who realize their need for him, for the Kingdom of Heaven is given to them.

God blesses those who mourn, for they will be comforted.

God blesses those who are gentle and lowly, for the whole earth will belong to them.

God blesses those who are hungry and thirsty for justice, for they will receive it in full.

God blesses those who are merciful, for they will be shown mercy. God blesses those whose hearts are pure for the they will see God.

God blesses those who work for peace, for they will be called the children of God. God blesses those who are persecuted because they live for God, for the Kingdom of Heaven is theirs.

"God blesses you when you are mocked and persecuted and lied about because you are my followers. Be happy about it! Be very Glad! For a great reward awaits you in heaven. And remember, the ancient prophets were persecuted, too. Matthew 5:3-12

When we live for Jesus whom has saved us. Saved us from a world that is filled with sin. Satan no longer owns us Jesus has paid the price for us and bought us back for God. God's plan is for us is to be with him for eternity, and through Jesus this has been made possible. When we come to the cross and lay our sins, we humble ourselves to God. We want to let go of our old life and live for Him.

To have a heart of complete transformation of Jesus, we will not look at the world messages, we will see right through them. The messages of the world will always be there to tempt us, but when our hearts are transformed with Jesus we become strengthened. We become filled with the Holy Spirit.

We begin to see that true happiness is within our hearts that are filled with the Love of Christ. When Jesus lives within our hearts, it is then the transformation will begin to produce the fruits of the spirit. The Fruits of the Spirit are love, joy, peace, patience, kindness, goodness, faithfulness, gentleness, and self-control.

The abundant life that we are to live comes from within, with Jesus in the centre of our hearts. Abundance of good comes, when we have all good in our heart. That is the seed we plant within us that produces an abundance of life.

Our world is a fast paced environment that trains us to take short cuts when we want to, and when we do live this way we treat others poorly. This is what are sinful nature is trained to do. It is selfish and only reacts to our flesh needs.

Our human nature is to be, fast paced. When we let God in through Jesus, we are guided by the Holy Spirit.

In order to have compassion for one another, we must have it within ourselves. We look at the cross to understand the love that God has for us. Gods love through Jesus is seeing the Glorious God that he truly is.

What a person reflects on the outside is what is in the inside. When we see each other react to certain situations in life, we see that who truly is happy and who is not.

Jesus understands the pains that we go through. He understands the shame that you carry. Jesus was sent to earth for the purpose of dying for your sins. Jesus Christ is the Saviour of the world.

The day of his crucifixion he was rejected. He was beaten, spit on, whipped, laughed at. People filled the streets shouting "CRUCIFY HIM!".

He was rejected by the world and was put to death on the cross for us. Even today he is being rejected by many in our world.

Even the Disciples said that is is very hard to understand, and questioned how can anyone accept it?

Many of his Disciples turned away and deserted him. Twelve remained.

Jesus was rejected. He understands. He knows what it feels like.

Everyone goes through rejection. Rejection is painful from whomever it comes from. It is how we handle ourselves afterwards that is important.

In living a right relationship with God, I have been given a joy for life. I am now remarried to a man that has the same love for God, and also walks in the right relationship with God.

In growing in a relationship with Jesus Christ, Jesus protects you from rejections in life. Jesus comforts you when you are rejected, and you become strengthened in his love.

God sacrificed his son Jesus so we can be close to him. He will never reject us, and that is the truth that we can trust. Our creator loves us so much that he gave us the gift of eternal life.

In scripture:

For God so loved the world that he gave his only begotten son that whosoever believeth in him should not perish but have everlasting life. John 3:16

God gave us his son. The only decision we have is to confess our sins and accept that Jesus died for our sins so we can be close to God. God says to come to him through his son Jesus Christ, leave your baggage sin(shame) at the cross. God will take it from you. You release it to him and he will renew you. Jesus is the good seed and when we focus on the message and take it in to our heart we will be transformed and renewed a right spirit.

God knows rejection, and He has open arms for all. God loves unconditionally.

The rejection brings so much shame into our lives. The pain of rejection brings the feelings of being unworthy, alone, hurt, anger, sadness and so much more. Shame brings these negative thoughts, and we often beat ourselves up mentally which is not from God.

When we bring it to the cross, we leave the shame at the cross with Jesus. He carries it for us. He cleanses us, so we can be made right to be in the presence of God.

Jesus takes the imperfections from us, and breaks the bondage that it has on us. Jesus made it possible to be in the presence of God and to be able to call him our Father. When we accept the gift God has given us in his son, we are than made worthy to be his children.

The day Jesus was put to death on the cross one of the Roman Officers that had led him to his death and nailed him to the cross, was one of the mockers of Jesus. The officer witnessed Jesus taking his last breath. Before Jesus took his last breath Jesus shouted out to God to forgive them for they do not know what they are doing. The moment Jesus died the curtain in the Temple was torn in two, from top to bottom. The Roman officer stood facing Jesus and watched him die exclaimed "Truly this was the Son of God!"

He saw the glory of God that day. He felt the shame of rejecting Jesus. In Luke it states that he praised God. He turned away from his shame in that hour of Jesus death.

When we recognize that Jesus is the way, and we glorify God, we are united with God.

Jesus will not reject you, and he will not reject your baggage of sin. He is ready and willing to take all of your shame exchange it for beauty.

Glory to God for the unconditional love He has shown us when He gave us the gift of His son Jesus Christ.

All we are asked is to say "YES God, I believe in your son Jesus". Accept him into your heart and believe Jesus lives.

Praise be to God. Forever and ever.

FORGIVENESS

"If you forgive those who sin against you your heavenly Father will forgive you. But if you refuse to forgive others, your Father will not forgive your sins." Matthew 6:14-15

Forgiveness is for all who come to Jesus. We must forgive others as we have been forgiven by God.

Peter asked Jesus how often should we forgive someone who sins against him. Seven Times? Jesus replied "Seventy times seven".

Wow, it is quite clear that Jesus states that forgiveness goes a long way. We are commanded to forgive.

In scripture:

Then Peter came to him and asked, "Lord, how often should I forgive someone who sins against me? Seven times?"

"No, not seven times," Jesus replied, "but seventy times seven![

"Therefore, the Kingdom of Heaven can be compared to a king who decided to bring his accounts up to date with servants who had borrowed money from him. In the process, one of his debtors was brought in who owed him millions of dollars. He couldn't pay, so his master ordered that he be sold—along with his wife, his children, and everything he owned—to pay the debt.

"But the man fell down before his master and begged him, 'Please, be patient with me, and I will pay it all.' Then his master was filled with pity for him, and he released him and forgave his debt.

"But when the man left the king, he went to a fellow servant who owed him a few thousand dollars. He grabbed him by the throat and demanded instant payment.

"His fellow servant fell down before him and begged for a little more time. 'Be patient with me, and I will pay it,' he pleaded. But his creditor wouldn't wait. He had the man arrested and put in prison until the debt could be paid in full.

"When some of the other servants saw this, they were very upset. They went to the king and told him everything that had happened. Then the king called in the man he had forgiven and said, 'You evil servant! I forgave you that tremendous debt because you pleaded with me. Shouldn't you have mercy on your fellow servant, just as I had mercy on you?' Then the angry king sent the man to prison to be tortured until he had paid his entire debt.

"That's what my heavenly Father will do to you if you refuse to forgive your brothers and sisters from your heart."
Matthew 18: 21-35

God instructs us that we must have mercy when someone wrongs us. We should overflow with mercy towards others, Just as God is towards us.

When we read this scripture my first thought was how can a wrong of a rape, murder or abuse be forgiven over a wrong of being called a name, talked about through gossip, stealing or telling a white lie.

You see God does not measure sin. A sin is a wrong and we are all sinners. God wants our hearts to be free from sin so by not forgiving we are sinning. When we don't forgive our hearts become hardened with anger, hurt, frustration, emptiness and so many more thoughts that are not of God. These thoughts empower us and that is what distances us from God our Creator.

God is Holy. God is all good. That is why Jesus was sent to die on the cross for us. We are sinners, and God is complete Holiness. To be in Gods presence, we must be washed of our sin. When we come to him asking for forgiveness, we are asking God to take the sin in our lives away so we can be drawn close to him.

Now, God does not want you to be in pain and anger through your life, so he asks you to forgive just as he forgives you through the sacrifice of his son Jesus Christ.

In Matthew 6:14-15 Jesus explains when you forgive others God will forgive you, If you refuse to forgive others he will also refuse to forgive you for your sins.

When we live a life filled with sin, we can't be close to God because he is holy and pure. In heaven there is no room for sin. That is the purpose of Jesus death on the Cross. We are made one with God through Jesus.

Our time on earth should be spent making our hearts right with God. We are being prepared to enter into the Heavenly Kingdom. Our hearts need to be cleansed, and the only way that can happen is through the blood that was shed by Jesus on the Cross.

Forgiving others is not for the one that has done the wrong it is for the one that has been wronged against. It is to keep us close to God. To have a close relationship with God we must be willing to keep our heart clean from sin. It is only then that we can come closer to God and have a growing relationship with him.

It is for our good that we continue to give ourselves to God. We are the ones that are not perfect, so when we come to God we are cleansing the imperfection in us. When are hearts are humbled, we are admitting that we are sinners, and are not perfect. When we walk with God in a relationship with Jesus it is then that we become moulded to the person we are to be for God. We become more like Jesus.

A good thought to keep in your mind would be "what would Jesus do?" Ask yourself that question each time you need to make a decision. As well decisions can be prayed about, and referenced back to the Word of God. What does scripture tell us on this issue? When we go to God for the answers, He will guide us. Living for God is also being obedient to his decision. We will talk more on obedience later on.

Our human nature is to sin, so only through the giving of ourselves will we be able to walk a righteous path. On a daily basis give ourselves to God. We humble ourselves to him, recognizing that we can not live without God in our lives.

We also learn to forgive ourselves, as well as asking for forgiveness from the one we wronged. This process makes us right with God.

If you have wronged another it is good to make it right with that person. In a circumstance where that person has passed on in death, or moved away making it hard to reach this person. Making it right with God through forgiveness is okay. God looks at the heart of a person. God knows your heart, and through prayer you bring it to God. God can see the heart, and an honest heart is pleasing to God.

In Scripture:

God blesses those whose hearts are pure, for they will see God. Matthew 5:8

Shame brings darkness. Our emotions can take control of us. When these emotions take control of our our life it separates us from God. God is Holy. When we clear our hearts from the sin we can release the shame. The emotions of anger, envy, fear, everything that is not of God can be released. We become closer to God. We let go of the shame and we release the power it has on us and are drawn in to Gods power of Love.

You can't do it alone. Jesus died on the Cross for all the reasons that is stopping you from really living life. If we carry the sin or live in the sin of our lives we bring in all the bad thoughts and feelings into our life.

In scripture:

> *When you follow the desires of your sinful nature, your lives will produce these evil results: sexual immorality, impure thoughts, eagerness, for lustful pleasure, idolatry, participation in demonic activities, hostility, quarrelling, jealousy, outbursts of anger, selfish ambition, divisions, the feeling that everyone is wrong except those in your own little group, envy, drunkenness, wild parties, and other kinds of sin. Let me tell you again, as I have before, that anyone living that sort of life will not inherit the kingdom of God. Galations 5:19-21*

A person had once stated to me that they could not submit their life over to God. They had a problem of someone else controlling their life. They couldn't fathom giving up the control of their life over to someone. Especially, to someone they cant physically see. When I asked "well how is your life going"? They paused and said "not so great."

When we live in shame and listen to all the negative thoughts that come from shame we are living in lies. Our sinful nature listed in the above scripture stops us from being close to God. The shame is keeping us from inheriting the Kingdom of God.

We are intended to live an abundant life, It is each of us that is choosing not to live it.

The Kingdom Of God comes from within us. When we have Jesus inside of our hearts the Kingdom of God will be opened to us. Jesus is the way to the Kingdom of God.

When we think of submitting our life to Jesus Christ we think we are giving up our identity which is not the case. We are surrendering our lives to walk a life like Jesus. Which gives us a close relationship with God. When we walk in a relationship with God we inherit the Kingdom of God. In the Kingdom there is abundance.

God loves all that come to him in the name of Jesus.

In Scripture:

At that time you won't need to ask me for anything. The truth is, you can go directly to the Father and ask him, and he will grant your request because you use my name. You haven't done this before. Ask, using my name, and you will receive, and you will have abundant joy. John 16:23-24

When we go to the cross where Jesus carried the sin of the world, Jesus speaks on our behalf to God our Father.

Jesus is God in the flesh. God really knows what you are going through or what you have gone through. God knows what is like to be rejected, he knows your hurts and and all the wrongs.

God came down to this earth through Jesus to bear the sin of the world.

Jesus walked this earth and brought the message to his disciples for us to hear the message today. God has a plan for each and everyone of us.

Humble yourself to God. Proclaim to God that you are ready for him to take away the burden that you are carrying, and live a life of abundance through Jesus. Jesus is the Heir to the Kingdom of Heaven. The Kingdom of Heaven is for us, when we accept the truth who Jesus is.

With God all things are possible. God is bigger than your issues, and he can handle any size of problem. Nothing is to small or to great for God to handle.

In Scripture:

Grieve, mourn and wail. Change your laughter to mourning and your joy to gloom. Humble yourselves before the Lord, and he will lift you up. James 4:9-10

The above scripture speaks of how God will hear the heart of one whom come to him and he will lift them up. Will you hang onto ashes or have God turn ashes into beauty in your life?

God loves us so much that he has offered us a choice of the sacrifice of his Son Jesus Christ. That is the free will God has given us. The choice to follow him.

The choice of freedom is on the Cross, and we are given a choice to accept.

God has given you a gift, the choice you make can change your life for eternity.

Prayer

Dear God,

I am a sinner, and I know that I have done wrong. Please forgive me for my sins. I ask that Jesus come into my heart, and renew a right spirit in me. Thank you, Jesus for dying for my sins and I acknowledge that you are the Living Son of God. I know that I am not deserving of your forgiveness, but because of the Grace of God, I am saved. I want to spend eternity with you in Heaven.

In Jesus name, Amen.

Glory to God.

OBEDIENCE

---

*He replied, "But even more blessed are all who hear the
word of God and put it into practise." Luke 11:28*

The Israelites had a really hard time being obedient to God when
we look back at scriptures. When we look at today society we see
that in many ways it is the same.

In the Bible God showed them many miracles for the Israelites
to see in broad day light.

I am referring to the story of Moses in the Bible.

Moses was chosen by God to lead the Israelites out of Egypt
and into the Promised Land. The Promised land was the land that
God had promised to his chosen people. A land filled with milk and
honey. This land was to be beautiful, and to the Israelites whom had
been slaves, this land was everything and more then they could have
hoped for. Moses had a hard task, but it was all possible because
God was in control.

The journey was long when the Israelites were being lead to the
Promise Land. The journey was long but worthwhile.

The Israelites were people that had complained and had little
faith. They never seemed to be happy.

The Israelites were lead out of Egypt by Moses from Pharaohs'
captivity. God instructed Moses to guide the Israelites out of
slavery.

Moses had convinced Pharaoh to let them go through the
many miracles God had performed through Moses, and the many

wrath's that God had put upon Pharaoh. Pharaoh I believe became exhausted and felt that his Gods that were in fact statues or idols were no match to Moses living God.

The Israelites were rejoicing when they found out that Moses was leading them out of captivity to the Promised Land.

The Israelites were rejoicing when they were let free. They were witnesses to many of the miracles that had been performed by God through Moses. God's power was visible to their eyes.

The Israelites had gathered all their live stock, belongings, and their children and journeyed out of Egypt. They were lead out of Captivity from Pharaoh that kept them from living a free life.

After they had been travelling for awhile now out of Egypt, Pharaoh had changed his mind. Pharaoh wanted the Israelites back to do his work, he wanted the Israelites to be his slaves. He had gathered many of his soldiers with him and chased after them.

In a distance, Moses and the Israelites had seen Pharaohs men come after them in their chariots.

The Israelites screamed and panicked. Often that is the case with our lives today. When we don't see something go smoothly we tend to panic. We worry and doubt in our situations, and faith seems to dwindle.

Moses whom was leading them had faith in God, and had called out to God for guidance. God had opened the Red Sea forming a wall of water to two sides, and a path down the middle. I am sure it was an amazing sight to see.

As the Israelites had moved down into the sea in the dry path to the other side. God placed a blazing ball of fire in front of Pharaohs men to stall them so they could not get closer to Moses, and the Israelites.

The Israelites were instructed by Moses to move into the dry path of the Red Sea with the walls of water held back by God. God held Pharaoh and his soldiers back by putting a blazing ball of fire in their path.

When the the blazing ball of fire went out, Pharaoh and his men continued on their chase to get the Israelites.

When all the Israelites where safely on the other side of the Red Sea, they could see that Pharaohs men were still coming after them.

Again, the Israelites had panicked that Pharaohs men were gaining on them. The Israelites, had witnessed God releasing the walls of water, as the, water poured out over Pharaohs men as they had crossed the Red Sea. The Red Sea had swallowed Pharaohs men. The Israelites felt freedom once again.

The Israelites panicked, even when they saw a miracle of water being held back to leave a path for them. God was with them, helping them free from slavery and all they could do is panic and complain that Pharaohs men were catching up to them.

How often do we complain about our circumstances in our lives? How often do we make bad choices and when we do we sulk about them grumbling how unhappy we are? Our thoughts are to focus on our God and what his promises are.

God performed a miracle before their eyes, and all they focused on was the fact that Pharaohs men were catching up. As well, they focused on the food that they were missing as slaves in Egypt. We must focus on God and what his promises are. To be obedient in God is rewarding. God never changes, it is us that changes.

He said he would free the Israelites from captivity. He promised Moses that he was going to be with them to help them to the promised land. God fulfilled his promise.

He brought them to the other side of the Red Sea completely dry. God is in control at all times. When we focus on him, and are obedient to God, we will not be distracted by the surroundings of the world.

I often thought about how God feels when we make the same mistake over and over. We are constantly moving, and more often we are moving away from him instead of toward him. We don't keep our focus on his promises. To be obedient to God is to follow through and know that God has kept his promises always. God never changes.

When we focus on God by setting time in prayer and devotions we allow ourselves to be filled by him instead of the worries of the world.

God has created us. He knows everything about you. He knew you before you were born. He knows how your story of life unfolds.

We are given choices and it is through the choices we make that are life will unfold.

We are busy complaining sometimes to see the wonderful plan that God has for us. It is when we seek him and are obedient to his word God reveals our purpose and the meaning of life.

When I think of God and how he knew me before I was born. He knows my failures and successes. He knows my path of life.

God desires to have a relationship with us. When we want to know more about God and have a relationship with him we discover the abundant life he has planned for us.

To know that we can walk with God in a relationship and to have access to the Kingdom of Heaven on earth is amazing. He gives us free will to follow him, and through that choice, we live an abundant life on earth. We are blessed with Gods Grace.

God created us in his image. In each of us we have a part of God. When we have Jesus Christ in our lives, and we focus on getting to know him we open up this overflowing love inside of us that is ready to be unleashed in our lives.

When we come to the Creator God through his son Jesus, he opens the doors to knowledge and wisdom. A life of abundance.

God opens our eyes when we come to know him through his word and prayer. He created us to be with Him, to live with Him now, until eternity. A plan that we could walk and talk with God. We can have a relationship with Him.

The Israelites showed weakness and bitterness on many occasions. When they did not see things go their way they complained. They did not trust that God was leading Moses. They did not see what was in the future for them. All the Israelites focused on was that they were hungry and tired.

We often live in the "we want it now" mentality. The difference is how we approach the Now. We must live now praising God. Change now your belief. Change now your obedience to God.

When we are being disobedient we are then not on a clear path to our abundant life that we are intended to live. Disobedience brings in the wants which is a demanding "Now". We want to be obedient to God and be confident in our "Now I have peace".

In Scripture:

> *If you love Me, obey my commandments and I will ask the Father and he will give you another counsellor, who will never leave you he is the Holy Spirit, who leads into all truth. Jesus goes on to say that the world at large cannot receive him, because it isn't looking for him. But you do, because he lives with you now and later will be in you. No I will not abandon you as orphans—I will come to you. John 14:15-30*

Jesus spoke very clearly that those who seek him will be provided with the Holy Spirit as a Counsellor. Jesus promises the Holy Spirit if we obey his commandments.

When we love Jesus and follow his commandments we are walking with God. The Holy spirit helps us lead into all truth.

We will recognize the Holy Spirit when we are following Jesus, and we grow in our spirit with him.

God never left us alone. His plan was for us to be with him, but obedience in him leads us to the truth and being in His very presence.

I learnt that surrendering to God is an everyday choice. A choice we make to live as a loving obedient servant to God. We can not do it alone and God knows that. He sacrificed his son so we don't have to be alone.

Now, God never said that life would be easy but he did say we will never be alone. God never changes, He is always there for us.

Our sinful human nature changes. We are forever battling with our sinful nature.

God had created us in his image. And since God created us in his image we have God given qualities within us. When we open our heart to God, and are obedient to his commandments, we are living a pleasing life for God.

We will then truly experience a relationship of growth in spirit through Christ. When we hunger and thirst for God He will fill you up with truth. The Will of God is for us to follow Him with all that we have.

Will you live your life serving God by living a life that is pleasing to Him.

Have obedience in Him and say "May God your will be done, not mine".

Glory to God!

PATIENCE

Be humble and gentle. Be patient with each other, making allowance for each other's faults because of your love.
Ephesians 4:2

In Exodus God guides the Israelites from slavery. I took note that he brought them the long way. Why the long way? When we travel we take the shortest route possible either to conserve on gas or we are just so anxious to get there. I found it intriguing that God took them the long way. What was the purpose of the long way?

The Israelites were on foot and had sandals to walk in. They did not walk with Canadian Footwear shoes that had really comfortable soles. They were taken the long route, bare feet in sandals.

How many times have we prayed to God, only to find our selves asking why aren't things changing? In fact, in our prayer life we are actually asking why are you taking so long God?

God takes us the long way to teach us patience. It is true what they say patience is a virtue. It really is. Most people struggle with patience. With perseverance I believe God teaches us to have patience. God can change matters in the blink of an eye, but then if he did that every time, his children would not learn a thing. That is when I truly understand that God loves us, by teaching us to be patient. The whole purpose in having patience is to have faith and trust in him.

What happens when we have a long journey through troubles we get impatient, we are tempted to complain and resist. Just like the Israelites did. They had complained that they were tired and hungry. They had been tempted to go back to Pharaoh and give up their freedom for a meal.

We need to trust in these times which will build us in our relationship with the very God who knows our limits. He knows what is in the future for us, and He works all things out for the good.

We need to put our trust in Jesus who is at the centre of our hearts that will guide us through our troubles. Yes, it is a learning process to continue to submit to the Lord Jesus Christ in all situations. We must learn to submit to the Lord Jesus, so we can follow Gods way.

We can not do it alone. God knows that, and that is why he came in human form in His very own Son Jesus to show us that we are to trust Him in all things.

When the Israelites were being lead to the Promised Land by Moses they had grumbled and complained. They questioned the God that was freeing them from slavery. It was taking to long, they were hungry, they were thirsty, they questioned this God of Moses. I can imagine how Moses felt as he was leading them. His patience must have been heavily tested with the complaints of the people.

If God would have brought the Israelites directly to the promised land they would not have seen Gods work through His miracles. They would not have witnessed the miracles and seeing how powerful God really is. We would not be reading them in scripture today.

As well the Israelites needed to learn to have faith. They would not have been taught a whole lot in how to believe, Complaining shows how weak their faith really was.

As parents we are always teaching our children patience. How can you teach patience, when one does not have patience.

It is through our trials and our weakest moments that is when God strengthens us, and does his best work in us.

When we are being lead the long way it may not be the path we want to take. God has chosen it for us, and he knows what is best for us. We must strive to have patience in our lives.

When we choose to meddle in His way, the path only gets longer. We are choosing to make it longer.

We are to learn to be still. It is when we are quiet and still that we learn patience. We are strengthened then in our faith.

In Scripture:

"Be still and know that I am God!
I will be honored by every nation.
I will be honoured throughout the world." Psalm 46:10

I want you to reflect on your own life. Reflect on times where you could have had more patience. Ask yourself am I patient?

To really have patience we learn from the Word of God. When we look at the example Jesus showed us in his walk on earth, he was a man that had time for everyone.

In the bible we can reflect on scriptures about patience.

Luke 15:11-24
Romans 8:24-30
1 Corinthians 13:4
Galations 5:22
Ephesians 4:2
2 Thessalonians 1:4-5
Hebrews 11:13-16

One of the scripture that shows a reflection on Gods patience. How God patiently waits for his lost children to return to him is in Luke 15:11-24. I encourage you to read these scriptures, and ask God to give you wisdom in reading His Word.

To find a quiet place and still your mind, and really listen to the stillness. That is where you will become intimate with God.

God waits for us to come to him. He watches over us, and waits for us to knock on his door.

Prayer

Dear God, help me to be still and quiet in your presence. In Jesus Name Amen.

PURPOSE

For I know the plans I have for you," says the Lord. "They are plans for good and not for disaster, to give you a future and a hope. Jeremiah 29:11

Where am I? Who am I? Why am I here? What is the purpose of life? What is the purpose of my life?

I realized that shame in someone's life can take over, and lead a persons life into a journey through misery and despair.

Shame overpowers thoughts, and brings a person to look at them selves in a critical way. Shame, if left inside a person can grow into very destructive thoughts, and shape a person. Shame stops a person from being the very person they are intended to be.

When my ex-husband rejected me and divorced me I had put my self worth in his hands. I allowed the thoughts of rejection take over and I shaped myself in those thoughts. I now look at things differently. My purpose was not to live my life for him. It was to live for God.

Did you know that you do have a purpose, and the only one stopping you from living it is you. Yes, you.

When we believe in the love of God, through his son Jesus, our purpose will come more clear.

When we know we are loved by God, we know we are created in his image, We know we have Jesus in our Hearts, we know we are given the Heavenly Kingdom.

Gods love is incredible, and when we truly understand that within ourselves we will feel ourselves change. Remember Gods Love is not just a feeling. Love can be felt in an emotion, but Gods Love is unconditional so it just is. God is Love.

When I was rejected by my ex-husband I was being lead by my feelings. All negative thoughts were flowing through me. That is not truth. That is not God.

Often we love someone for what they have done. Gods Love is Unconditional, and is always present. It is the purest love ever. It is referred to the Agape Love. Which means a self sacrifice love. It never stops, it never changes, it just is. God is love.

God does not stop loving you when you sin. Gods Love is always overflowing.

Our Human nature is sometimes we stop loving, because we are tired of a relationship. That is why we have divorce. And that is why divorce is not what God desires for us.

Gods love conquers all. That is truth, that Gods love conquers all. Without Gods love we are nothing. With out Gods love you and I would not exist. Gods love just is, and does not measure.

The greatest commandment of God is to love him with all your heart, and all your soul, and all your mind, and with all your strength. The second, is to love your neighbour as yourself. God commands us to love, because God is love and to have that power within you brings you abundance of joy in your life. God loves us so so much he does not command it to hurt us, but to guide us to keep us from getting hurt.

If everyone in this world would love we would live in a better world, but man changed it when we invited sin in our lives.

When we focus on Jesus, we bring the Love of God into our lives and we become a beacon of light of love.

When we become a beacon of light of love we are a living lantern for God. The purpose of our God given talents come out as we strive to live a God honouring life.

To live a God honouring life we have to be careful with the seeds we plant in our minds. You see when we have shame in our life from sin we are filling our minds with everything that is not of God.

When we read Gods word we fill our minds with truth.

Jesus spoke of the seed in scripture through parables.

Parables are stories in which he taught. He taught hidden truth in these parables to the one whom seeks a better life. The hidden truths only come visible to the seeker of Jesus.

In Scripture:

"A farmer went out to plant some seed. As he scattered it across his field, some seeds fell on a foot path, and the birds came and ate them. Other seeds fell on shallow soil with underlying rock. The plants sprang up quickly, but they soon wilted beneath the hot sun and died because the roots had no nourishment in this shallow soil. Other seeds fell among thorns that shot up and choked out the tender blades. But some seed fell on fertile soil and produced a crop that was thirty, sixty and even a hundred times as much as had been planted. Anyone who is willing to hear should listen and understand!"

His disciples came and asked "why do you always tell stories when you talk to the people?"

Then he explained to them, "You have been permitted to understand the secrets of the Kingdom of Heaven, but others have not. To those who are open to my teaching, more understanding will be given, and they will have an abundance of Knowledge. But to those who are not listening, even what they have will be taken away from them. That is why I tell these stories, because people see what I do, but they don't really see. They hear what I say, but they don't really hear, and they don't understand. Matthew 13:3-13

What seed have you been planting? The seed we plant are what we believe in our thoughts. What are we planting in our minds.

In Scripture:

"Now here is the explanation of the story I told about the farmer sowing grain: The seed that fell on the hard path represents those who hear the Good News about the Kingdom and don't understand it. Then the evil one comes and snatches the seed away from their hearts. The rocky soil represents those who hear the message and receive it with joy. But like young plants in such soil, their roots don't go very deep. At first they get along fine, but they wilt as soon as they have problems or are persecuted because they believe the word. The thorny ground represents those who hear and accept the Good News, but all too quickly the message is crowded out by the cares of this life and the lure of wealth, so no crop s produced. The good soil represent the hearts of those who truly accept God's message and produce a huge harvest—thirty, sixty, or even a hundred times as much as been planted." Matthew 13:18-23

Jesus speaks to us about his message that he has come to give life to the world. He came with a message, to let us know to look to him. Plant seeds that will root, not be snatched away from the evil one whom is Satan. Satan will come in many ways to disguise himself to keep you away from the truth, that Jesus is salvation and is the only way to the Kingdom of God.

There may be a circumstance in your life that has prevented you from experiencing joy in your life. The seed that Jesus speaks of is what we are to plant in our minds.

Whatever the circumstance is whether it is growing up in an abusive relationship, a tragic event that has happened in your life, by someone whom has wronged you in any way or maybe you have wronged another.

Whatever, it may be, you have the right to change it. You have the right to claim happiness, joy, and live life to the fullest. Plant good seeds, plant good thoughts. What you plant is what you will believe, and the thoughts that you believe in is what you will bring into your life. Jesus teaches us that mediation on the word of God is the most powerful seed. Read scripture when we wake in the morning, and before we go to bed. These times are the best times to cleanse our heart, mind and soul. To wake up with God, and close the day with God gives us protection from the worries of the day.

Everyone, has a story in their life, it is how you want to live it from this point forward is your choice. You can stay right where you are as a forever victim, or you can journey forward into a rewarding life of joy, happiness, and have an abundant life.

We make the choices in our life. Even if you have been wronged in any relationship you can over come it. When we choose not to live in the shame, and choose love we change the path of our life. The seed of thought must change. It begins with Jesus.

Now, that is where we go wrong in our lives, we concentrate on the very situation that has distracted us from the enjoyment of life. We concentrate on the shame.

I know it is hard to get past the deep secrets in our lives. We often go back to it, through our thoughts. Think about how many times you think of that horrible moment in your life that brings you to tears. Often brings out the very anger that grips you to make you spiral. These thoughts of shame can bring a person into addictions like over indulging in eating, over spending in shopping, over indulging in alcohol, drugs, sex addictions. The addiction brings the same feeling of shame that grips us. The addiction brings us into a deep well of shame and despair. We thought it would make us better but it gave us a moment of pleasure.

The world offers quick fixes. That is exactly what it is a quick fix, but it will never change you completely.

How can we stop from doing that? How can we let go?

I am going to tell you right now, that it does take work. When you do let go of shame everything that is attached to shame will go with it. All the negative/bad feelings that are attached to shame are anger, frustration, bitterness, envy, and feeling unworthy. It is also a change in your every day lifestyle.

I worked through the many thoughts of shame. I to felt all the negative feelings listed above, but I was tired of the path that shame was bringing me. I changed my bad thoughts to good thoughts. It takes commitment and repetitive positive affirmations to plant the positive thoughts.

You have to remember you planted the negative for a length of time. Now, you have to undo what is done. You need to reverse the negative that you planted, and replace it with positive affirmations. Jesus is the example to follow. Jesus honoured God with his life, and God was pleased.

We tend to blame others in our life which keeps us in a darkness. I have seen it time and time again. People unhappy with their life, and they are still blaming people from their past. You are only hurting yourself If you continue to blame.

When we come to God it is when we are desperate. Our world has fallen apart and now we need him. Yes, of course we need him. We need him always, but it is when We are desperate that we call upon him. I learnt that when we are at our weakest times, is when we call upon God, and it is than when we want God to do this miracle in our lives.

God allows us to come to that level because he then can do his greatest work in us.

God wants us to desire him, but not just in desperation. God wants us to have a relationship with him. Think of it this way, you may already have a friend now that only calls you when they need something. They are exhausting people, and they tend to walk all over you.

God does not work that way, every time we come to him he is there to listen. He wants to take the pain of shame away. God is there in your desperation, but he does his greatest work in you when you give him your time.

I poured my heart out to God on many occasions. Every time I am reminded how much we really need him.

We are not to hang on to the shame, God takes it from us through the love he has for us. That is why he sent us his son Jesus to die on the cross for us to live a life with him. His purpose was always to be close to us, and through that relationship, he will show us the very gifts we have inside of each an everyone of us.

Everything that comes in a negative thought is not from God. We make the choice to accept it or reject it.

In Scripture:

God showed how much he loved us by sending his only Son into the world so that we might have eternal life through him. This is real love. It is not that we loved God, but that he loved us first and sent his Son as a sacrifice to take away our sins. 1 John 4:9-10

Its incredible! We don't deserve it, but we are worthy to God.

In Scripture:

We know how much God loves us, and we have put our trust in him. God is love, and all who live in love live in God, and God lives in them. And as we live in God, our love grows more perfect. So we will not be afraid on the day of judgment, but we can face him with confidence because we are like Christ here in this world. 1 John 4:16-17

We often don't come to God because we are not perfect like Jesus, but we don't have to be perfect. God knows that we are not perfect, that is why he sent his son. Through his son Jesus is the only way to be accepted in Gods family. Through the acceptance of Jesus into our lives.

God sacrificed his only son to die on the cross, so we can have a relationship with him. We are made right with God through Jesus.

Jesus carried the burden of sin of the world and he nailed it to the cross for generations. It is done, he took the sin of the world and conquered it so shame has no more power upon us. Sin has no power over us.

Paul a servant of God pleads with us to sacrifice ourselves to God.

In Scripture:

"And so, dear brothers and sisters, I plead with you to give your bodies to God. Let them be a living and holy sacrifice—the kind he will accept. When you think of what he has done for you, is this too much to ask? Don't copy the behaviour and customs of this world, but let God transform you into a new person by changing the way you think. Then you will know what God wants you to do, and you will know how good and pleasing and perfect his will really is."
Romans 12:1-2 (our purpose)

Gods will is perfect. By choosing to live for God we are sacrificing ourselves to him. We are closing ourselves from all things around us that distract us from having a good life.

When we are centred with Jesus Christ we are welcome into the family of Christ. We don't let the world distract us from what is good.

That does not mean that you will not have problems. It means you will be able to have an inner peace with God that keeps you on the right path. You will be able to come to God in prayer and trust that he is there. You will experience the joy in life when you are living day to day. You will than be guided into knowing your purpose in life. You will live a life that serves your Heavenly Father. You will serve him willingly. Jesus will help and guide you through the difficult times in your life.

Everything comes from God. The house you live in, the car you drive, the money you receive from your career. Everything belongs to God.

God owns everything. He is the creator of our Universe, whom made us all in his image and has designed this beautiful plan that we all have the ability to choose.

Seek God who created us to live a life of abundance. He will provide inner peace, happiness and harmony.

Don't let the shame of where you are at in life lead you anymore. Claim the Freedom of Gods love through Jesus Christ. There is freedom in Christ. When you recognize the freedom in Christ, your purpose will come clear.

Repeat this prayer and claim your happiness.

> *Dear God,*
>
> *I want to come to know you through your Son Jesus who died for me on the Cross. I have not lived a life for you the way I have been living. I believe that Jesus is your Son, and died for my sins. I ask Jesus into my heart and ask that you forgive me for . . .*
>
> *I don't want to live in bondage to shame. I release it to you, because I have chosen today to live for you and only you.*
>
> *In Jesus name I pray Amen.*

Prayers are love letters to God, and through a sincere heart God hears his children call on him.

Glory to God in the Highest.

GRATITUDE

Be thankful in all circumstances, for this is God's will for you who belong to Christ Jesus. 1 Thessalonians 5:18

Your attitude can make or break almost any situation. Your energy is what you bring. You can decide to be negative and complain, or be positive and be thankful.

If you change your attitude you change your life.

In Scripture:

Always be full of joy in the Lord. I say it again—rejoice! Let everyone see that you are considerate in all you do. Remember, the Lord is coming soon. Don't worry about anything; instead, pray about everything. Tell God what you need, and thank him for all he has done. Then you will experience God's peace, which exceeds anything we can understand. His peace will guard your hearts and minds as you live in Christ Jesus.

And now, dear brothers and sisters, one final thing. Fix your thoughts on what is true, and honorable, and right, and pure, and lovely, and admirable. Think about things that are excellent and worthy of praise. Keep putting into practice all you learned and received from me—everything

> *you heard from me and saw me doing. Then the God of*
> *peace will be with you. Philipians 4:4-9*

Through my greatest despair in life, I became depressed from the ways of the world. I came to realize when we are filled with gratitude we change who we are. We want to look to God through our gratitude.

Look around you. Look at what God created. When was the last time you smelled the roses, taken a walk in nature and appreciated what is around you. The birds singing, the sky how blue it is, the moon and stars, how vibrant the sun is. God is everywhere.

When we focus on our circumstances going on in our life, we tend to be overwhelmed by a dark cloud. We must look past the circumstance and focus on Jesus. That is what Jesus did, he kept his eyes on God. He looked past the darkness in our world. He looked past the unbelievers that would not listen to his ways. He prayed, and gave gratitude to God. He kept focus on living out the will of God.

I was frustrated, angry, sad, bitter and so unhappy with all the details in my life. I was lacking so much in my life, and it was through this despair that I came to know the greatest gift in the world. Jesus.

I have come to know God through his Son Jesus Christ. I have come to know God through his love, that changed my life completely.

Through my prayers of distress, I had picked up my Bible to unfold the most beautiful relationship, that brought me joy, happiness, patience, and abundance in life. I began to live with a renewed spirit that kept growing from the wisdom and knowledge of getting to know Jesus.

I was carrying the very power of Jesus inside of me. When I called on Jesus, and I asked him again into my life. I discovered him in a new light. and was filled up with his goodness.

I started realizing that my thoughts were controlling what was happening in my life. I was bringing misery into my life because all

I thought of was how unhappy I was. I was unhappy because of my circumstances.

When we let go of the stuff which is the new car, house, career, money, etc. And focus on Jesus we gain much more than what material things offer us.

When I filled my thoughts of unhappiness, I was just getting more of unhappiness. It started to make sense that my thoughts were what was keeping me from living.

God says that you reap what you sow. I was in shock that now in my greatest despair, I realized that it was my fault that I was here, not God's. I was reaping what I had sown.

A negative person will always attract more negative circumstances into their life if they continue on that path. When I looked at people around me, I saw the revealing truth.

When I looked at my life, and how I had married a man that treated me with no respect, I was battling my self worth. My life felt like I was always racing, and getting no where. Like a hamster on the wheel.

God desires for us to have an abundant life. He desires us to have all the riches of his kingdom. He does not want us to struggle in life. He wants us to understand our need for him. He did not design life for us to fail. He designed this great plan only for us to succeed.

When we feel the bumps in the road, tell him. When we experience doubt, tell him. When we hurt in our painful decision, tell him.

It is our decision where we want to be in life. It is our thoughts that create the decisions we make.

God loves everyone, and through God's way there is understanding. God is a personable God. God is all knowing.

That means there is nothing you can do or not do that will make him love you more. He loves no matter what. God Is all love. We can not earn his love, by doing good deeds. God does not work that way. God loves.

God Loves everyone. We are all sinners, and he loves each and everyone of us. Yes, he even loves people that choose not to follow him, he does not approve of how they are living their life, but none the less, he loves them. That is why Gods Love is unconditional. He is love.

We are all called to the cross, but if we do not believe in the son of God whom is Jesus Christ we can not be one with God.

Who ever comes to the Father in the name of Jesus Christ has been given rights to the Kingdom of Heaven.

Jesus is the key to salvation. Jesus has inherited everything from God. When we come to God through Jesus we are brothers or sisters with Jesus Christ and we are called Gods children.

We can call him Father and are included in the inheritance that he has given authority to Jesus.

In Scripture:

"My Father has given me authority over everything. No one really knows the Son except the Father, and no one really know the Father except the Son and those to whom the Son chooses to reveal him". Matthew 11:27

In Scripture:

One day the Pharisees asked Jesus "when will the Kingdom of God come?"

Jesus replied, "The Kingdom of God isn't ushered in with visible signs." You won't be able to say, 'Here it is!' or 'Its over there!' For the Kingdom of God is among you." Luke 17:20-21

Gods Kingdom is within our hearts! Gods Kingdom is when we accept Jesus in our hearts and truly believe that the Son of God Is Jesus. Jesus walked the earth to spread the love of God, and tell us this beautiful plan that God has for us.

Paul whom lived by the power of Jesus living within him taught the value of the Kingdom of God.

In Scripture:

For the Kingdom of God is not just fancy talk; it is living by God's power. Which do you choose? Should I come with punishment and scolding, or should I come with quiet love and gentleness? 1 Corinthians 4:20-21

Jesus stretched his arms out to people as he taught his followers. He prepared his disciples to go on into this world. He knows our hearts, and by our hearts we are chosen to come into the Kingdom of God.

We carry the Kingdom of Heaven within us, but it is by Jesus Christ whom enters our hearts that allows us have access to the Kingdom.

Jesus is the beginning of the renewing of your heart. We must think of what is good, and replace all our negative thoughts with gratitude and praise. Jesus the greatest teacher is our example.

Jesus came into this world to bring peace, joy, harmony and abundance. He did not come to condemn the world. Jesus lived his life as an example for us.

When we ask Jesus into our lives he sends the Holy Spirit to guide us. He is to be the centre of our hearts which perfects our love.

In each and everyone we have a gift and when we access the gift that God has placed in our hearts, your life will be filled with abundance.

When I learnt this truth, I realized that Gods love is deeper and wider than we can ever imagine.

To have the greatest joy is to serve the God of the universe, and he provides the necessities of life through his blessings.

Give Gratitude to yourself, admire your own features. Embrace yourself by admiring your qualities. Stand in front of a mirror and admire your beauty. Thank God for you eyes, your nose, the freckles he placed on your face, admire you.

Gratitude, to the creator of you. You will see amazing things happen.

Most people criticize themselves, and what they are actually doing is criticizing God whom is the creator of you.

When you admire yourself, you will see your self-confidence grow, and you will become a strong, vibrant person with a glow of energy.

A Grateful heart sings praises to God. When we have heart filled with gratitude it keeps us close in our relationship with God.

Praise be to God.

BELIEVE

"At last the time has come!" he announced. "The Kingdom of God is near! Turn from your sins and believe this Good News!" Mark 1:15

What a person believes in will shape who you are.

We Bring up our children to believe they can be anything they want to be. When they are young, their imaginations run wild.

When My son was younger he pretended he was a dinosaur. He was a raptor, and had the walk of a T-Rex down to a tee. He had his hands and the hunch of the meat eating carnivore down pat. His roar was out of this world.

When he was a little older at an age when we knew he could handle watching the movies of Jurassic Park. We allowed him to watch. It was even more exciting because he got to see these creatures on a big screen.

As my son grew up, he had this amazing imagination that was so intriguing to watch.

His imagination grew to discover dinosaur bones in our back yard. He wanted to be a paleontologist. He was excited at a young age as he believed. In his imagination he was in fact a paleontologist. He believed!

When Jesus was teaching we read in Matthew 19:13-15. That some children were brought to Jesus so he could lay hands on them and pray for them. Parents wanted their children to be blessed by Jesus. That is a big deal. Can you imagine how these parents must have felt when they were in the presence of Jesus, and to have an opportunity to have your children blessed.

To have your children blessed by Jesus in their life was a big deal. The children were being blessed. These children were given a blessing by the living God. They were going to succeed in life.

The disciples of Jesus said to the parents not to bother him. Jesus responded "let the children come to me. Don't stop them! For the Kingdom of Heaven belong to such as these". Then he put his hands upon them and blessed them.

Jesus blessed the children in front of those parents. We need to understand what Jesus is saying that "Let the children come to me". He knew that the children know how to use their imagination, which made believing easier for them.

When we are children our minds are open to teachings easier than when we are adults. We learn so much more. When we are children we live by using our imagination. We learn how to eat, walk, and play at a young age. We move on to school, and we learn to interact with others. As we get older we change in our ways. As we grow up we become hardened and set in our ways.

It is when we are reaching High School Graduation that we decide what we want to do with our life. We choose to continue on in education or continue with the family business.

Our parents, friends, teachers, co-workers are now giving their feed back on life. Our thoughts are formed by the feed back we receive from others. That information is now in our thoughts, and we make our decisions in life from the information we have learnt from all these other people that have touched our lives.

When we are kids we believe and we play with our imaginations. We believe we can be anything we want to be when we are children.

We can be whatever we want to be. We can fly a plane, become a doctor, a fireman, a policeman where ever our imagination takes us. Once we stop playing with our imagination we really end up crushing our dreams and goals.

The desires of our heart is what makes us believe. We as children want to be a dinosaur we act. If we want to be paleontologist we are one in the moment. Whatever it is that day, we are what we believe.

When Jesus says let the children come to me, he knew that the children believed in him. Jesus knew their hearts are in the right place because a child like belief is what we need to grow our faith in him. The children are innocent and pure when they believe with all their hearts.

We must enter the Kingdom with a child like imagination, because than our hearts are not hardened.

We need to find ourselves through Jesus. When we look to Jesus for who we are, we discover the beauty of our purpose.

In Scripture:

For if you confess with your mouth that Jesus is Lord and believe in your heart that God raised him from the dead, you will be saved. For it is by believing in your heart that you are made right with God, and it is by confessing with your mouth that you are saved. As the Scriptures tell us, "Anyone who believes in him will not be disappointed." Romans 10:9-11

To believe we must recognize Jesus. To believe we have the blood of Jesus whom is Truth cleanse us, and it is than that we can act in faith.

In Scripture:

When Jesus arrived Capernaum, a Roman officer came and pleaded with him, "Lord, my young servant lies in bed, paralyzed and racked with pain."

Jesus said, "I will come and heal him."

Then the officer said, "Lord, I am not worthy to have you come into my home. Just say the word from where you are, and my servant will be healed! I know, because I am under the authority of my superior officers and I have authority

*over my soldiers. I only need to say, 'Go', and they go, or
'Come', and they come. And if I say to my slaves, 'Do this'
or 'that', they do it."*

*When Jesus heard this, he was amazed. Turning to the
crowd, he said, "I tell you the truth, I haven't seen faith
like this in all the land of Israel! And I tell you this, that
many Gentiles will come from all over the world and sit
down with Abraham, Isaac, and Jacob at the feast in the
Kingdom of Heaven. But many Israelites—those for whom
the Kingdom was prepared will be cast into outer darkness,
where there will be weeping and gnashing of teeth.'*

*Then Jesus said to the Roman officer, "Go on home. What
you have believed has happened." And the young servant
was healed that same hour. Matthew 8:5-13*

This Roman Soldier believed that Jesus could heal his servant by
just asking. He did not need for Jesus to come with him physically
to his servant.

Jesus was amazed with the Roman Soldier. The Roman Soldier
believed. The Roman Soldier believed that his servant was healed
from Jesus without physically seeing it.

When we believe in the unseen this is what we call faith. Jesus
saw that he believed and he healed his servant from a far. To believe
your heart, mind and soul are united in your belief.

In Scripture:

*What is faith? It is the confident assurance that what we
hope for is going to happen. It is the evidence of things we
cannot yet see. Hebrews 11:1*

Glory to God for his Faithfulness.

TRUST

Trust in the Lord always, for the Lord is the eternal Rock.
Isaiah 26:4

As a friend you may have told a friend that they were to trust you. Maybe you screamed at your parents "trust me", when they laid a curfew down. Either way the words "trust me" has been most likely been in your vocabulary sometime or another.

Trust is valuable in a relationship and when we break the trust it is a stumbling block. Sometimes when trust is broken the relationship comes to an end.

When I became a christian I had this spirit of goodness in me. Each time I prayed I had this joy in my voice and I can feel this excitement that was so real. I felt good, but as I continued on my journey as a christian I found that trust was something I was not good at.

How do I trust God with my life? It sounds simple but our human nature isn't to trust so easily. Trust should not be hard but it is for us. We change and that is natural on our part, but God never changes.

God has a plan for each and everyone of us, and trust is a big factor in our relationship with God. We can be easily swayed when something goes wrong.

In Scripture:

I am sure that God, who began the good work within you, will continue his work until it is finally finished on that day when Christ Jesus comes back again. Phillipians 1:6

God allows obstacles in our lives that will teach us how to trust.

What is the first thing when we find that trust has been broken with one of our children. We discipline them by not allowing them to continue with that behaviour. God our Heavenly Father does the same for us, he disciplines according to our actions. God does not mess up. We do.

We give him our lives and than we wait, but we get impatient. So we try to help God along. That is when we wander off the path.

When we pray to God and give him authority over us, we must allow him to work. Trust God to do the work. We must trust him in all things. God is faithful always.

God always works things according to his plan. Not our plan. God knows our heart, we can't hide from him. He knows if we are trusting him.

God can be trusted in all things. Now, of course you can't say God "I trust you will let me win the lottery this week". God can not be manipulated or tested. God can be trusted to help you live the purpose given life. When we trust God in our lives we than begin to see our faith grow immensely.

Can you imagine following your children around all the time because you didn't trust them. What kind of relationship would you have with them? You most likely would end up pushing them away and have no relationship at all. To make matters worse your children would grow up with not trusting in there relationships and so it would be passed down into the relationships they try to build.

Trust can be abused and when trust is abused in a physical or sexual matter, there are Counsellors that can help mend the brokenness one carries in these circumstances.

I encourage you to get help if you have been a victim in a physical or sexual abuse. Nothing is to big for God. We are welcome to the

Cross, and he is ready to take the burden from you. Don't let the lies of Satan whom delights in a person feeling weak and helpless. When shame leads us to not reach for help through a counsellor it prevents us from walking with God. God wants you in a right relationship with him. Reach out for help through someone you can trust.

We need to make the choice in our life. You can do it, you can let go of shame, and trust again.

Nothing can separate us from Christ's love. In his Love we can trust that we are loved by our Father as we are. Come just as you are.

In Scripture:

Who shall separate us from the love of Christ? Shall trouble or hardship or persecution or famine or nakedness or danger or sword? As it is written:

"For your sake we face death all day long; we are considered as sheep to be slaughtered."

No, in all these things we are more than conquerors through him who loved us. For I am convinced that neither death nor life, neither angels nor demons, neither the present nor the future, nor any powers, neither height nor depth, nor anything else in all creation, will be able to separate us from the love of God that is in Christ Jesus our Lord. Romans 8:35-39

We will never be alone because victory was won in Christ. Praise God!! Alleluia!

FAITH

What is faith? It is the confident assurance that what we hope for is going to happen. It is the evidence of things we cannot yet see. Hebrews 11:1

One morning as I drove to church that Sunday morning the air was crisp and fresh. As I was driving fog filled the air. I reflected at this as a true relationship with Christ. When we submit our life we can't see what is ahead of us. As I was driving the lines on the road were guiding me. I could see ahead only a about a car length in front.

The lines stood for what Christ is in my life, my guidance, keeping me centred. Jesus is my friend walking with me keeping me centred in my journey in life.

When I looked in the rear view mirror, I could not see anything. That represented my sin that he took on the cross with him. I was forgiven and the record of my sin was gone. God has erased my past.

When we look to the cross and reflect at what Christ accomplished on that cross we can move forward. Christ offers freedom to all. God loves us, and he desires us to have this open relationship with him.

Understand that God is here, and Jesus his son is the doorway to a life filled with abundance of joy, peace, happiness, and so much more.

In Scripture:

Just then a woman who had been subject to bleeding for twelve years came up behind him and touched the edge of his cloak. She said to herself, "If I only touch his cloak, I will be healed."

Jesus turned and saw her. "Take heart, daughter," he said, "your faith has healed you." And the woman was healed at that moment. Matthew 9:20-22

The above verse speaks of a woman who touched the cloak of Jesus when He was talking to a leader of a synagogue. What happened next was amazing. When the woman touched him (Jesus), he felt power being released. Jesus said to the woman "your faith has healed you". And the woman was healed at that moment.

Jesus felt the power come out of him, and knew her thought. That women had faith, and by her faith she was healed.

Our thoughts are what is powerful, and gives us our faith, or lack of. What we think about we bring about. This woman's thoughts were of Jesus and what he had was power to heal and by her faith she had took action to get close to him. Jesus holds the power. When we fill ourselves with Jesus, we have that power within us.

Understand that when we persevere in our life we accomplish, and we succeed. Think about it, if you want something you go for it.

This woman thought, and she acted. Through the power of Jesus Christ and by faith she believed and she succeeded. The woman succeeded through her faith in Jesus Christ.

When we give up, we bring thoughts of unhappiness, and start bringing our self worth down. We start knocking others that have it, and we become negative, and we beat ourselves up about it. Our thoughts are what we begin to believe and we end up sulking and sometimes bring ourselves into a depression.

Now, the woman that touched Jesus robe made an effort to change it. She was determined to touch Jesus, and she changed her life forever. You can too.

Now, Jesus is not here in the flesh, but He is here in spirit and that is where it begins. Have faith in Jesus.

Jesus takes the ashes and turns it into beauty. Jesus the Son of God is completely powerful and by the acceptance of him, and what He has to offer is life changing.

Living life with out Jesus, I had gone through a painful divorce. I felt rejected, and hurt. I made the decision to bring that pain to Jesus, and walked through my valley of pain. Having faith in Jesus at the time to help me get through it was rewarding. I grew in my relationship with Him, and he transformed me by my faith in Him. Jesus continues to do great things in me. We must have faith.

Be willing to give up your stuff. I mean, the stuff inside of you that is making you feel bad. The hurt, the pain, the loneliness, the jealousy, the self-worthlessness, the self-pity, the anger, the frustration, and all the bad feelings that are stopping you from feeling the joy in life.

I wanted to live again, and Jesus gives life. We are in a better place when we keep are eyes on Him.

Jesus lived by His faith in his walk on earth. He preached the importance to have faith. He was a man that showed his state of being.

Positive emotional state brings happiness. Jesus was always positive. Jesus had faith in God.

Negative emotional state brings depression. Jesus cast out sickness, and disease. Which comes from lack of faith.

Jesus had warned his disciples of negative thoughts in scripture. He explained negative thoughts are like yeast. Yeast spreads and grows.

> *In Scripture: But the disciples discovered they had forgotten to bring any food, so there was only one loaf of bread with them in the boat.*

> *As they were crossing the lake, Jesus warned them, "Beware of the yeast of the Pharisees and of Herod."*

*They decided he was saying this because they hadn't brought
any bread. Jesus knew what they were thinking, so he said,
"Why are you so worried about having no food? Won't you
ever learn or understand? Are your hearts too hard to take
it in? "You have eyes—can't you see? You have ears—can't
you hear? Don't you remember anything at all? What about
the five thousand men I fed with five loaves of bread? How
many baskets of leftovers did you pick up afterward?"*

"Twelve", they said.

*"And when I fed the four thousand with seven loaves, how
many large baskets of leftovers did you pick up?"*

"Seven," they said.

*"Don't you understand even yet?" he asked them. Mark
8:14-21*

Jesus wanted them to understand that negative thoughts are
dangerous. The Pharisees hearts were hardened.

Jesus knew the disciples thoughts, and knew they did not
understand his warning.

Watch what you listen to. Guard your heart by what you take in.

When we look at Jesus, and what he represented. He represents
Freedom from our sins. He is good, he is glorious, he is holy, he is
perfect, he is joy, he is patience, he is love.

Jesus had crowds around of people who wanted to see him, and
hear him. He spoke of love, and how to get it. He healed the sick,
he cast out demons, he raised the dead, and brought hope into this
world.

Jesus taught and prepared his disciples to go out into the world
and teach "truth". Because "truth will set you free".

To bring truth into your life, we look to the teachings of Jesus.

What we believe in is what we shape our lives on. We become
what we are thinking.

Did you know you can tell a child that they are stupid, and they will grow to believe this false lie about them self and fill their life with negativity and shape there life around this belief. The reason why, because they believe that it is the truth.

You can believe a negative is truth, so basically people can believe that lies are the truth.

We must be very conscious of the power of words in our lives. What we believe in, can shape us.

Now, Jesus taught us in his teachings that positive thoughts are what we should be concentrating on. The truth will set us free, and we find that in His teachings.

In Scripture:

Finally, brothers and sisters, whatever is true, whatever is noble, whatever is right, whatever is pure, whatever is lovely, whatever is admirable—if anything is excellent or praiseworthy—think about such things. Whatever you have learned or received or heard from me, or seen in me—put it into practice. And the God of peace will be with you. Phillipians 4:8-9

The above scripture we read about fixing our thoughts on what is true and honourable and right. Think about things that are pure and lovely and admirable. Think about things that are excellent and worthy of praise.

By doing this in practice in are daily life with God, He will bring Peace. God will bring peace into our lives when we fill our mind and heart of good thoughts. Reading Gods word is meditation for the heart, mind and soul.

When we let our desires consume us in thought we can get frustrated, and not go about it the right way. When desires consume us we are filled with negative thoughts.

When Jesus is in our thoughts we live in the light. When we fill our hearts with the word of God, we begin to transform our minds like Christ. We are than controlled by the Holy Spirit.

Live life by releasing the negative, and strive for being better. Let go through prayer, areas in your life that make you feel weak.

When we bring positive affirmations into our lives through the word of God we are transformed by the power of God.

When we are positive we are producing good energy. We become better within ourselves and we can accomplish so much more in life.

We will live in peace, joy, and harmony with our selves and with others. God is in each of our hearts and when we draw on power from God we become stronger in our faith.

We are called to live in harmony with God, and when we put into practice the prayers, meditations and affirmations we will attract into our lives abundance. When we put into our mind and heart goodness we will receive goodness.

Grow to love God, you will than grow to love life. Life will then love you back. God will transform you. Others will see you as this positive light, and they will want to be apart of it.

Darkness gives negative thoughts, Light gives positive thoughts. We become what we think about.

When we read about Jesus in the Bible we read that he had followers. People gathered to meet him. He had crowds of people around him. He was a well loved man, and people wanted to be in his presence. He was the and still is the light of the world, and that light is what attracted so many to him. They wanted to be saved from their life. They knew that Jesus was special. They witnessed it. They felt it. So they came.

The ones that rejected him were filled with fears and anxieties. Their hearts were hardened towards him, so they had all the negative thoughts fill there minds. They refused to believe that Gods son was walking among them. Their fears kept them from believing in Jesus. Their fears kept them from the abundance that God desires us to have.

God designed life, and it is through our thoughts that we become close to him. God is Holy, and being holy there is no negative thoughts. That is why you become distant to God when you listen to your negative thoughts.

Jesus brings truth in everything. Jesus brought the people truth. Truth is all knowing.

Jesus speaks of the Holy Spirit whom is our counsellor that guides us.

In Scripture:

But the fruit of the Spirit is love, joy, peace, forbearance, kindness, goodness, faithfulness, gentleness and self-control. Against such things there is no law. Those who belong to Christ Jesus have crucified the flesh with its passions and desires. Galations 5:22-24

When we are guided by he Holy Spirit we are walking with Jesus and are close with God.

In Scripture:

Do not be deceived: God cannot be mocked. A man reaps what he sows. Whoever sows to please their flesh, from the flesh will reap destruction; whoever sows to please the Spirit, from the Spirit will reap eternal life. Let us not become weary in doing good, for at the proper time we will reap a harvest if we do not give up. Therefore, as we have opportunity, let us do good to all people, especially to those who belong to the family of believers. Galations 6:7-10

In the above scripture we read that we reap what we sow. If you have thoughts of negative, you will reap from the negative thoughts.

The key here is that God can not be deceived. God sees the heart of a person. A person may think something, but if your heart is not in harmony of what you are thinking than it is useless.

You will reap what you sow, so it comes down to what you believe and what is in the heart.

When you express yourself with love, you will bring so much more into your life. Love, love, love. That is the most important commandment.

God loves us unconditionally, he does not stop loving when we don't love him.

That is who God is. God is love. That is why we must love God first.

When we give ourselves to God, and grow to please him we will reap eternal life. We continue to do good, and good with a heart that honours God will reap a harvest.

Negative, you will reap more of negative. Positive you will reap more of positive in your life. The choice is given to each of us, and when we choose to have faith in God, we will reap a harvest of abundance into our lives.

To have faith in God, is by recognizing Jesus. Jesus recognized God when he walked this earth. Jesus now sits on the right side of God and is the heir to the Kingdom of Heaven.

Glory to God for his faithfulness.

LOVE

"God so Loved the world he gave his one and only Son, Son that whoever believes in him shall not perish but have eternal life." John 3:16.

We build a relationship with someone before we can fall in love with them. Well when we think of Jesus we must do the same.

When we are told about Jesus we know that this is a man that served God. We know that he is holy, and represents all that is good.

When we build a relationship with Jesus we come to understand the love He has for us. We can't expect to know him if we don't build a relationship with Him. Reading the Word of God is where we hear the amazing stories of Jesus and His work for the Father.

In Scripture:

Love is patient and kind. Love is not Jealous or boastful or proud or rude. Love does not demand its own way. Love is not irritable and it keeps no record of when it has been wronged. It is never glad about injustice but rejoices whenever the truth wins out. Love never gives up, never loses faith, is always hopeful, and endures through every circumstances. Love will last forever, but prophecy and speaking in unknown languages and special knowledge will all disappear.

The greatest gift is Love. 1 Corinthians 13:4-8

Understanding Gods Love while I was going through a lot of troubles in my life was difficult. A painful relationship that lead me to a divorce. I found myself in debt by spending money on senseless material things, as well as I was searching for something to bring me joy through my career choices. I did not gain in any of those things because I now realize what it means when God says don't place your trust in the world, but in Him.

When I struggled through these difficult times in my life, I asked the question what I wanted. I want a good life.

Through this time in my life, I got down on my knees and asked God what is it that I am not doing right? Why is my life not working the way I wanted it.

My answer did not come out of the sky with an audible voice. With thunder and lightening as sound affects. I believe most people believe God is, harsh, and demanding.

The more I came to God, the more my eyes were opened to him. I persevered him, and submitted my everything to him.

When you surrender everything to God and let him know that you need Him. We humble ourselves to God and accept his ways. We open our heart, mind and soul to Gods way. Submitting your everything to God, is humbling your everything to him. You release your life to him.

God created everything, through his love. God shows us that through love all things are possible. God is love. Everything is possible with God.

Jesus is the answer. Believe that God sacrificed Jesus, Gods only son to die on the cross for our sin. Gods love is real.

In Scripture:

"God so Loved the world he gave his one and only Son, Son that whoever believes in him shall not perish but have eternal life." John 3:16.

When you have a relationship with someone both people contribute. Meaning, you get to know each other. When you are dating you are in this aura of excitement because you are discovering each other.

When one stops giving in a relationship, the relationship ends up dyeing out. Many people today settle in their relationships and are very miserable. They stay together for the children. All they are teaching their children is to stay in an unhealthy relationship.

A relationship is an investment. You spend time getting to know one another. When we stop investing you end up fizzling. You invest your time. When you nurture the relationship you become closer.

You don't look at the relationship what can I get out of it, you start a relationship with what can I give.

I remarried to a wonderful man. We had many ups and downs, but because of our investment towards each other we keep our love alive. We are able to be happy in our relationship and can pass on to our children the joy of loving one another.

In Scripture:

> *Jesus replied, 'You must love the Lord your God with all your heart, all your soul, and all your mind.' This is the first and greatest commandment. A second is equally important: 'Love your neighbor as yourself.' All the other commandments and all the demand of the prophets are based on these two commandments." Matthew 22:37-40*

When you put God first in your life and other relationships next, you are opening your life to beautiful relationships.

How you build on your relationship is what you are going to receive in your relationship. You build each other up. You continue to walk together in the same direction. Spending time together, and keeping romance alive.

God is first, and other relationships come next. God provides in all areas of your life, that is including in your relationships.

When we give our priority to God He gives us the love in our life that is from Him. The love that loves unconditional.

Jesus being the centre of our heart, is what is pleasing to God. Walking with Jesus is what brings love into every aspect of our life.

That we can have success in all areas of our lives. In our finances, relationships, and career in all that we do. Through Loving Jesus we are close to God. God will than provide the Holy Spirit.

In Scripture:

The Spirit of God, who raised Jesus from the dead, lives in you. And just as he raised Christ from the dead, he will give life to your mortal body by this same Spirit living within you. Romans 8:11

But when the Holy spirit controls our lives he will produce this kind of fruit in us. Love, joy peace, patience kindness, goodness, faithfulness, gentleness, and self-control. Here there is no conflict with the law. Galations 5:22-23

Those who belong to Christ Jesus have nailed the passions and desires of their sinful nature to his cross and crucified them there. If we are living now by the Holy Spirit, let us follow the Holy Spirit's leading in every part of our lives. Let us not become conceited, or irritate one another, or be jealous of one another. Galatians 5:24-25

For this reason I kneel before the Father, from whom every family in heaven and on earth derives its name. I pray that out of his glorious riches he may strengthen you with power through his Spirit in your inner being, so that Christ may dwell in your hearts through faith. And I pray that you, being rooted and established in love, may have power, together with all the Lord's holy people, to grasp how wide and long and high and deep is the love of Christ, and to know this love that surpasses knowledge—that you may be filled to the measure of all the fullness of God.

Now to him who is able to do immeasurably more than all we ask or imagine, according to his power that is at work within us, to him be glory in the church and in Christ Jesus throughout all generations, for ever and ever! Amen. Ephesians 3:14-21

Paul prays to the Ephesians that understanding of Gods love is revealed to them. We can take this message into our lives today.

When we submit to Christ and follow his ways we will experience the greatest love that can be revealed to us.

In Scripture:

Jesus replied, "The most important commandment is this: 'Listen, O Israel! The Lord our God is the one and only Lord. And you must love the Lord your God with all your heart, all your soul, all your mind, and all your strength.' The second is equally important: 'Love your neighbor as yourself.' No other commandment is greater than these." Mark 12:29-31

Why would God command us to love him? God is love, so by loving him we abide by him and are obedient to the one whom is God over everything and everyone. Gods love is greater than we can ever imagine and by loving him, all who belong to him will live a Christ filled life that is honouring to him.

We must be known for our love.

In Scripture:

And now I want to urge you, dear lady, that we should love one another. This is not a new commandment, but one we had from the the beginning. Love means doing what God has commanded us, and he has commanded us to love one another, just as you heard from the beginning. 2 John 1:5-6

When we love God with all our heart and soul, God will shine through us and we bring glory to him. We honour God when we love.

In scripture:

Don't just pretend to love others. Really love them. Hate what is wrong. Hold tightly to what is good. Love each other with genuine affection, and take delight in honoring each other. Never be lazy, but work hard and serve the Lord enthusiastically. Romans 12:9-11

There is no end to Gods love. We don't have to impress God to gain His love. He loves us unconditionally. He calls us to extend that love through his son Jesus Christ, that lives in us, when we confess our sins. God brings our love alive in Him when we focus on Jesus.

Gods love wipes out all the shame, so don't pass up the greatest love of all. God sacrificed his son for us to be reconciled to Him.

Say a love letter each day when you wake up and each night as you go to bed. Gods love will never break your heart. Gods love will change your heart to love more. And through Gods love is how you have an abundant life.

Glory to God in the Highest!

THE KINGDOM OF HEAVEN

Jesus replied, I assure you, no one can enter the Kingdom of God without being born of water and the Spirit. Humans can reproduce only human life, but the Holy Spirit gives birth to Spiritual life. John 3:5,6

The kingdom of Heaven is among each and everyone of us. We are entitled to it through Jesus Christ. We have been given this gift, and when we truly receive it within our heart we discover the greatest plan that God has designed. abundance of life.

We are to come to know the secret plan of God. When we read in Ephesians Chapter 3 about a Prisoner Paul whom shared the secret. Paul was a prisoner because they did not want him spreading this good news of Gods mysterious plan.

In scripture:

God's Mysterious Plan Revealed

When I think of all this, I, Paul, a prisoner of Christ Jesus for the benefit of you Gentiles . . . assuming, by the way, that you know God gave me the special responsibility of extending his grace to you Gentiles. As I briefly wrote earlier, God himself revealed his mysterious plan to me. As you read what I have written, you will understand my insight into this plan regarding Christ. God did not reveal it to previous generations, but now by his Spirit he has revealed it to his holy apostles and prophets.

And this is God's plan: Both Gentiles and Jews who believe the Good News share equally in the riches inherited by God's children. Both are part of the same body, and both enjoy the promise of blessings because they belong to Christ Jesus. By God's grace and mighty power, I have been given the privilege of serving him by spreading this Good News.

Though I am the least deserving of all God's people, he graciously gave me the privilege of telling the Gentiles about the endless treasures available to them in Christ. I was chosen to explain to everyone this mysterious plan that God, the Creator of all things, had kept secret from the beginning.

God's purpose in all this was to use the church to display his wisdom in its rich variety to all the unseen rulers and authorities in the heavenly places. This was his eternal plan, which he carried out through Christ Jesus our Lord.

Because of Christ and our faith in him, we can now come boldly and confidently into God's presence. So please don't lose heart because of my trials here. I am suffering for you, so you should feel honored.

Paul's Prayer for Spiritual Growth

When I think of all this, I fall to my knees and pray to the Father, the Creator of everything in heaven and on earth. I pray that from his glorious, unlimited resources he will empower you with inner strength through his Spirit. Then Christ will make his home in your hearts as you trust in him. Your roots will grow down into God's love and keep you strong. 18 And may you have the power to understand, as all God's people should, how wide, how long, how high, and how deep his love is. May you experience the love of Christ, though it is too great to understand fully. Then you will be made complete with all the fullness of life and power that comes from God.

Now all glory to God, who is able, through his mighty power at work within us, to accomplish infinitely more than we might ask or think. Glory to him in the church and in Christ Jesus through all generations forever and ever! Amen. Ephesians 3:1-21

When you make the choice to let go of the shame, and accept that Jesus is the way to the Heavenly Father. The doors will be opened, and Jesus will be waiting.

Clean your heart daily and walk in the light in believing that Jesus has conquered victory over sin.

You make the choice to believe in the truth who Jesus is and it is by the renewing of your heart, that he will transform your mind.

Jesus is the power to living an abundant life which you hold within yourself. When you believe in him, and walk with him a life of abundance is truly yours. The abundance lies within us through Christ. The choice is ours to want it. This is the free will of God.

There are many today choosing to walk through life living a life that is empty.

In Scripture:

"Keep on asking, and you will receive what you ask for. Keep on seeking, and you will find. Keep on knocking, and the door will be opened to you. For everyone who asks, receives. Everyone who seeks, finds. And to everyone who knocks, the door will be opened. Matthew 7:7-8

Through out scripture we are given the teachings of Jesus and we hear from many of the witnesses that had the experience with being with Jesus on this earth. Jesus died but he is very much alive. He has risen.

When we put to death our old self, and journey in a new life with Jesus Christ we enter into The Kingdom of Heaven.

In Scripture:

Jesus said to the people who believed in him, "You are truly my disciples if you keep obeying my teachings. And you will know the truth, and the truth will set you free." John 8:31-32

Glory to God in the Highest.

REVIEW

What you believe in is who you become, or how you live your life.

The seeds that you are planting within you are, are your very own thoughts.

We can over come failure by our reaction that proceeds.

When we are obedient to God we become aware of our purpose in life.

Living in gratitude for the things around us will only allow more to come into our lives.

Love conquers all, and through that love we can change into becoming the light that Jesus calls us to be. We bring our love into action.

When we forgive, we are letting go of the shame and all its grief to live a life of abundance which we were intended to live from the very beginning.

When we have patience we become stronger in who we are as Gods children.

Faith comes from walking in a right relationship with God, and it only comes from knowing the son of God, Jesus.

There is power in the name of Jesus Christ.

We find our Purpose in life when we seek the God who created us, and through that purpose we bring out our God given gifts.

God knows his creation "US". He desires for us to have a close relationship with him.

Gods plan from the very beginning was for us to live an abundant life with him.

The Kingdom of Heaven is within each of everyone of us, it is our choice to receive access to it.

Positive Affirmations from Scripture

Do not conform any longer to the pattern of this world, but be transformed by the renewing of your mind. Then you will be able to test and approve what God's will is—his good, pleasing and perfect will (Romans 12:2)

So whether you eat or drink or whatever you do, do it all for the glory of God (1 Corinthians 10:31)

Whatever is true, whatever is noble, whatever is right, whatever is pure, whatever is lovely whatever is admirable—if anything is excellent or praiseworthy think about such things. (Philippines 4:8)

We know that in all things God works for the good of those who love him and have been called according to his purpose. (Romans 8:28)

Give thanks for all circumstances, for this is God's will for you in Christ Jesus (1 Thessalonians 5:18)

For I know the plans I have for you, "declares the Lord "plans to prosper you and not harm you, plans to give you hope and a future. (Jeremiah 2:11)

My dear brother, take note of this: Everyone should be quick to listen, slow to speak, and slow to become angry, for a man's anger does not bring about the righteous life that God desires.
(James 1:19-20)

For we are God's workmanship, created in Christ Jesus to do good works, which God prepared in advance for us to do. (Ephesians 2:10)

Therefore do not worry about tomorrow, for tomorrow will worry about itself. Each days has enough trouble of its own. (Matthew 6:34)

You have the mind of Christ. (1 Corinthians 2:14)

He will give me the desires of my heart. (Psalm 37:4)

The Lord is with me; I will not be afraid. What can man do to me? (Psalm 118:6)

His divine power has given us everything we need for life and godliness through our knowledge of him who called us by his glory and goodness (2 Peter 1:3)

ABOUT THE AUTHOR

In her early fourties Beverly D. Wiebe a Canadian, wife and mother of two felt compelled to share the love of God. Through difficult chooses in her school years, a divorce, and a crushing depression she realized you don't need a bachelors degree to find Gods Love.

Her journey in finding herself opened up the truth of Gods Love.

Letting go of the shame from wrong decisions that lead to a painful divorce and depression. God brought a transformation of heart, mind and soul. A new life that has lead her to joy and freedom in Christ.

Through the Power of Gods Love all things are possible, and if he is for us, who can ever be against us. AMEN